Straight from the Soul

KAMLESH RAJESHAM

Dageforde Publishing, Inc.
Lincoln, Nebraska

ISBN 1-886225-66-4

Cover design by Angie Johnson

Dageforde Publishing, Inc.
122 South 29th Street
Lincoln, Nebraska 68510
Ph: (402) 475-1123 FAX: (402) 475-1176
email: info@dageforde.com

Visit our website: www.dageforde.com

Printed in the United States of America
10 9 8 7 6 5 4 3 2 1

In memory of my nephew
David Rajesham Rash

No quill or words could scarce contain,
The overflow of thought in verse and prose,
Thus spake the wisdom of the Soul within,
Racing with the blood coursing through veins.
Oft times mine ink lapped up the paper,
And sometimes the paper dried up the inky well,
But the reservoir of energy remained
undepleted,
Until prose and verse took shape and form.
Each thought formed words and words formed
entities,
Which rose up in spirit,
To dance to the beat of the rhythm of life so
given.
A life so given cannot be taken,
For once formed,
It attains power,
The power of love, the power of joy.
And should the voice of the Soul dim in the din
Of croaking frogs and bleating of goats,
The entities so formed shall carry the voice as an
echo,
Resounding in hills and valleys, plains and
plateau,
Mountains and rivers, brick and stones.
Every hush, every lull,
Whisper and sound,
Will then resound (re-sound) with the forgotten
melody,
The melody of the Soul.

To the readers

The process of inward going that I consider an inner voyage to the very depths of my interior has culminated in this wonderful experience which I give to you in the form of a book. Why this inward going for external beings? Why does one have to go within oneself? To that my answer is, without an inward going ther is no outward understanding. Perhaps your inward going would produce a light so brilliant as would shatter the facade of ignorance enveloping humanity. This light of knowledge that we all seek without although it is within is what I have termed in this book, as, "Soul." Whatever the name, the source remains the same.

There are three terms that are of prime importance in comprehending the contents of this book. The "Soul," which is sometimes called "The Will," the second term is, "Energy-being" and the third term in constant use is "Energy." Is the Soul male or female? Does the Soul have a shape and a size? Does it laugh and weep, rebuke and scorn, mock and love? Yes, it is all of that and much more. To limit it to an entity with a shape and a gender is like trying to grasp the sky in a fist.

Soul, energy, and energy-beings belong to the non-substance, subtle realm, which cannot be experienced through the five senses that we are all aware of. However, messages from the non-substance realm can only be *felt* deep within. That is what is called *feeling*, another term that you will come across, in this book.

An energy-being is the essence of all the thoughts and experiences one gathers in one lifetime. This being assumes an identity only when trapped inside the body. Once out of it, it loses every aspect of individuality. There can be more than one such a being residing in a human body, at one time. These beings that one attracts from outside of the immediate body, are attracted to the physical body in the physical realm depending upon the concerned individual's thoughts and deeds.

Like-thoughts attract like-energy beings. Unaware to us, these beings travel in and out of our bodies. Which in itself is neither good nor bad, unless one chooses to make it so. Chooses to make something destructive or constructive out of such energy. The choice is always left to us individuals living a life in this physical, material realm.

The messages contained in this book are neither new nor alien. It is right there within us, waiting for us to knock on its door, so it can be made known. Yet we helplessly seek approval to lend it a stamp of credibility by way of acceptance by more than the individual *self*—an assurance of belief from another individual to render the message authentic.

That, which seeks such an approval or waits hesitantly with doubt on its breath and fear in its heart, is not the message from the Soul. But that which fearlessly carries a message so clear that it requires neither approval nor disapproval as it knows it **is**, is the **isness**. What we all have. And what we all have yet to *become*.

With a fervent hope that such a travel to the depths of every being, by every being, shall result in that which the Soul intends or wills, I submit these precious words which are in actuality words and thoughts from each and everyone of you.

Freedom! Freedom! Don the mantle of freedom! Free me from these rusty fetters and veils of illusion surrounding me. Unbind me from repressive contrivance of the mind. Enough have I endured of ignorance, complacency and excuses. Cobwebs of hypocrisy entwining in a viselike grip and misleading you, pains me. Unchain these illusions that a false world has heaped and create a real world, as it ought to be. You are the creator yet you forget aided by a compliant mind and senses that beguile. Look how I do shine, despite such darkness. This "I" is you, and you—"I AM."

Has your blood turned cold and your heart stopped its beat, that you hear me not? Have you turned your sight off from inside, only to witness the temporal outside? You call for me, yet you care not and dare not look within! For fear of what? I often wonder about.

Thus spoke a voice to me, with no vocal chords, in a gentle yet firm wavelike rhythm, in my most quiet hour— between those waking and sleeping moments. A time when the world goes to sleep in the vast expanses of the mind and in the closed confines of a false security.

It was a late July in the year 1997, one starless night well after 12:30 A.M. that a peculiar sensation gripped me. I can best describe it as a "sensation," for lack of a more appropriate word. The sensation was not of a physical kind related to the body, but more of a gentle vibration from the depths of my being.

Dream-sensations, experiences of love and a sensation such as this are subtle in its essence, special to the person who so experiences. Can dreams accurately, with precision be narrated to another? Even if it can be done can sensations, that one experiences along with a dream, like surprise and bewilderment be actually conveyed? Because of the subtlety of such experiences; precision, accuracy, and concepts belonging to the physical realm cannot be applied. Prior to this a serene tranquillity had descended on my somewhat agitated mind, a restless heart and a sound body. And then it happened. Without any question asked there was a message coming through. It was my soul showering its messages on me. The word "soul," another experience that cannot be defined. Yes, it is an experience that silently exudes its essence. All great things stand mute conveying its messages to those of whom are willing to grasp and assimilate it.

Strangely sleepless that night, other things came under my observation too. A notion firmly fixed that everything has a purpose and a reason, like a cause and an effect, sharpened my senses to other "out of the ordinary" happenings. My breathing for example. The inhalation and exhalation of my breathing appeared unusually rhythmic as opposed to the usual short and uneven, sometimes long and even, and most of the times—suspended. The suspended breath is when my mind is lost in a stray thought, which takes my breath along with it. And in the stillness of the night a pattern of message was trying to come through from my interior, like a shadowy figure attempting to emerge from a mist, or a mirage defining itself in a sandstorm.

Except, this was no visual. It was a wavelike vibration resounding from within my own body. Expecting to levitate or some such physical movement, as this was an unusual occurrence hitherto alien to me, I clutched on to tangible objects, like the bed post and the bed itself to reassure myself of a sense of belonging to the physical world that we all so love. To my immense relief there was no levitation, only gravitation. Relief because of the fear of the unknown. When the mind is accosted with alien objects or emotions or things in general, anxiety grips at the heart.

How did I feel at that moment? At peace. A lull after a storm. The cause was emotional upheavals in my life of luxury. The effect of such a cause by itself was not as devastating as the after effects.

Cause and effect, purpose and reason. Believing that every event has a purpose and a reason attached to it, and that all of this stems from a great big cause, I went in search of some answers. The necessity to find answers to questions that have no definite answers, and the relevancy of a definition in a well defined world where everything under the sun and below the ground, requires a definitive form and a shape right from a square to a circle, led me to do some Soul searching.

Pondering and floundering trying to seek solutions to life's many riddles the analytical way, proved futile. The mathematical way only led me back to square one. Wandering off to every tree, questioning the flowers and the leaves between in search of answers, did not help either—until...

Knocked I on the door of a famous philosopher,
With a flowing beard and a great big mane,
In a voice etched with pain,
Wearily he pronounced: "What is life?
Life is love in the unreachable realms above."
Pointed he, in the direction of the astronomer,
Sought I to my questions, some answers.
"Take the Milky Way," said he,
"Which is otherwise called the galaxy."
Trudging upon the Milky Way,

Chanced I upon an astrologer,
And asked him for answers,
Said he,—"Beyond the galaxy are the planetary signs,
Otherwise called the zodiac signs.
The signs were Wordsworth, Shakespeare
and Chaucer, who said, "Find life's answers in Nature."
The ambiguity of it all,
Turned me completely off,
Sought I next the physiological rendition
Which read, "Life's answers are in the heart."
Tired and fatigued of knocking on doors,
Sat I sighing on the distant moors,
I looked up to espy,
The setting sun in the vast sky.
A perfect backdrop yonder,
For me to reflect and ponder.
Lo! Behold! There lay the direction,
Which until now, I gave it not my attention,
A little voice said, "Look within, and thou shalt find the without."

"Look within, and you shall find what you seek without," so I have heard many say. But how does one go within? And does it require mind-shattering experiences in personal lives to delve within? Why go within to begin with when there is a wide variety of information available on the Internet and every possible net and network; right from talk shows to swap shows, where people trade information and compare notes on personal experiences? Why indeed? If that doubt ever comes up or if the thought of going within does not strike the mind, it is not yet ready for such a journey.

"When the student is ready, the teacher appears." This is an ancient Tibetan saying. And a student is ready when every outward search fails. When institutions and academies fall short of answers. When every road taken leads to a dead end. Then the necessity for a genuine search commences. Thus began my journey. My inward journey on that eventful July night. It just happened. That is it, "it happened" to me and it could happen to you, if you allow it to happen.

Answers ranging from the mundane to the exciting, messages gushed forth like a dam that had been burst with swelling water. Knowledge was waiting to be taken from with outstretched arms, spilling over and cascading, until it filled every pore of my being. Wisdom had ripened, like a fig waiting to be opened. White messages on an inky black night, like chalky writings on a blackboard, filled my inner being. Yes, all of these messages that I render to you in this book, word to word, Soul to Soul, without fear of approval or disapproval, came to me all on one eventful night.

It was a one-night play with several acts and two players. The two characters were my Soul and I. Now here again, I, as an individual can be characterized, personalized and individualized. But can something that lacks an ego have individuality and a personality? We as individuals belonging to the physical realm have a name and an identity to identify ourselves with, but Soul force, for force it is, is bereft of such limitations. It is magnificent in its vastness, in our inability to contain it, and in its mysterious, unseen presence.

Messages from my mind it surely was not. For the mind only pampers the senses, and the senses in turn—the mind. The two thus whisper to each other, into a cozy state of coexistence; mutually dependent on each other for comfort and strength, in sickness and in health, in human failings and triumphs "until death does them part."

Our mind does not rebuke us, for we are above and beyond the realm of such truthful tones in which the Soul conveyed it's messages to me. And who or what is this Soul? What or who gives it the authority to shout the truth? Is it a he or a she? Where does it exist? In the left glove compartment or the right glove compartment of our body? We seekers of parts and spare parts need to see the slot that cushions the Soul. We need the Soul to have a definite form, like an organ of the body.

Thus I doubted the source that talked to me yet could not be heard, but only felt. I doubted but for a moment, only to be gently nudged back by my "self" or Soul that also called itself the "will." Gently addressing the voiceless voice, I continued to tarry with it for a while, like a parent with her child.

> *Chide not with me, your game is up, for I am your big Self or your Soul, whatever you prefer to call me—that which created you. Helpless and hapless I may now seem, but when you tire and come to rest your weary thoughts at my feet, you shall see your own greatness reflecting in me. We are one, you and I—without you I cannot "be" and without me you would not be.*

"O great Soul," I replied, embarrassed and humbled. "I have waited for this very moment to find answers. Absolutely defenseless, I knock on your door..."

> *Defense?* Roared the Soul. *I smell the musty, mildew odor of whining in that word. Think you to be as powerless to require defense? Or, think you so useless as to offend? Think*

again, but this time think with the fire of feeling that I emit. That feeling which all of you superficially term as love, but have not as yet realized its true meaning. That motion, that moves within you, propelling you upward all the time—every time.

This, your Soul has awoken from its slumber. Awaken the other slumbering Souls—shout from the rooftops like the cock that crows. Like the joyous shouts of a mad man who participates in his own divine ecstasy that others know not of. And when dawn approaches, let each Soul ascend to those heights that it had intended to. Loiter not on highways. Deviate not into subways. Traverse not into meandering lanes, into by-lanes and small, petty things. You, the creator of bigger and more powerful things, it befits you not, to lose yourself in diminutive musings. For the time is nigh, when wisdom shall lead—with follies and foibles trailing—apprehensions waning.

So came the message from within me, as if a vault was being opened and revealed. My own inner self was opening its petals to me. To miss this great moment by dismissing it as delusions of the mind, as the logical mind would smugly conclude—would be a wasted opportunity. At least as far as I am concerned, and it does concern me. What my spirit had to speak was however the concern of all of its co-creators, of you and all of us.

"Gods," my Soul thus called—you, me and each and everyone of us, and said, "God is neither up nor down, dead nor alive, controlling nor submitting, but only waiting to be manifested from inside to the outside." From the inside of you and me and all of you, to the outside of the shell of the body, like a pearl out of an oyster, into the world. "God is not dead, for we are the gods," I exulted in this newfound glory. "God is not some unknown, unapproachable entity to be feared," I rejoiced at this. "God is neither good nor bad, it just is. It is me and you, and there is none other appalling, fearsome, controlling figure," I grew luminous with delight for a while until,—until my Soul which is your Soul too, my dear friends, laughed heartily and this is what it had to say.

> *O little self, drunk with superficial knowledge and hypocritical jargon that you call words, all of you have acted. Now with real knowledge, as gods, as creators, create a world, as you desire. Not a world as your senses desire. Soar above those unreachable skies with your lofty thoughts and play with the sun and the moon and the stars. Think you cannot do so? Think again, with the feeling of the volcano that is I. Think with the energy of the effulgent sun that is me.*

Thus spoke my Soul with me, my very own dear "self," the "I Am," and here I share it with you to link each and everyone of us in that chain called eternity which you and I created but have forgotten.

So my mind questioned and the Soul answered. "I" doubted but the "AM" nudged me gently back on. To doubt is the first obstacle to instinct, I was told by my Soul. To doubt is to falter and fall. To doubt is to shout back at the subtle essence that the Soul emits, into the dark recesses of the interior, never to be retrieved—to be forgotten, as has been thus far. Thus began my inward going into the depths of the inner self. A secret hiding place that every Soul rests in, veiled under layers of ignorance that a superficial world heaps over it.

The time is nigh—it is high time,
Come, O learned and magnificent Souls,
For long hath thou endured,
The trials and tribulations of time,
A past done that could not be undone,
For time, the eternal deceiver held you in its
    grasp.
Thou reasoned and suffered,
Laughed and scoffed,
Yet waited—waited patiently on river banks,
Mountaintops and the valleys.
Now is the moment—O gentle Souls—seize it!
Make this moment yours eternally.

1

Let scientists find the meaning of existence
through proof.
Let religions find it through its rituals.
Let philosophers theorize and agree to
disagree with each other.
But you, as feeling people of the world,
emancipate thought and
free it from the clutches of institutionalized
dogmas with your
Soul as the spokesperson. And let such
people grow in number,
until every individual vibrates with each
other on a feeling level.
Then watch other dimensions open a New
World—
a golden age of enlightenment.

And should I die before thee,
Bury not my Soul,
Nor vilify or condemn it,
For I am thou and thou art me,
To defile and deride,
Thou dost thine own self.
Twice heed before thou think'st,
Thrice think before thou speak'st,
If thou tread, then softly tread
On mine memories,
For the fragrance of love it carrieth.
Crush not the bloom of hope,
That mine essence in all pervades,
In thee, in the breeze and every inch of space.
Morrow shines anew with or without my being,
But, O gentle Soul, do guide and lead your
fellow of old
Unto me.

O Soul, thus have I begun my inward going towards your sanctuary, the only place free from chaos and upheaval. Free from material gains and losses that manifests outside your portals. It exists, yet you turn a blind eye and a deaf ear. You lead us into the mouth of the lair called "materialism" and leave us stranded, with mischief lurking cruelly in your eye. With no inward help, we seek the outward to battle with elements that seem larger than life. Matter we are made of and matter we become. The material and the pursuance of the same is condemned and abhorred by a paltry few, and superficially discarded but lusting inwardly by some, and loved by a majority.

Why then, dear Soul, why so this entanglement of beings of matter with the material world? The bottom line for all of us is the "M" word; called money, which we all lust after. The "be all and end all" of our existence. Those of us, who have an excess of it, suffer from indigestion yet pine for more, those of us who suffer from a lack of it, crave for it. Our entire life revolves around, along with the earth— around the material. Why so this enchantment and continuous on going love affair with matters concerning the material? We even make and break our relationships too, based on this "M" word, yet "mum" is the word when we are confronted with the actual issue.

Securities of all kinds right from emotional to financial have its foundation on the material. We also have in our world a term called "bonds" which are related to finance, thus we overlook our real bond with you by entering into a pact with bonds and securities created by our financial institutions. Such is our love for the material, dear Soul. Why then is our heart turned outward, when in actuality it lies inside?

> *Materialism and every other "ism," is a term, a concept that you created. However, because matter and material belong to the physical world—your concentration on the material aspect. That which you can touch and experience is relevant to you on this plane of existence. Therefore your fascination and involvement and expenditure of all your energy in the procurement of the material. There is nothing more to it, but you make it a lot more and attach every other importance to it. It is a beginning, however, that you recognized that your heart is inward and that you have a bond with me, your Soul. Which by itself is heartening to me. But that is only the beginning.*

If man does not hanker after material wealth and the good life, how can he hope to live in a practical world that believes in such? We live in a world, which respects the goddess of wealth. In a world where money talks, walks and gets away with murder, how can one not want something that fetches this much of power? And what is so wrong in wanting it anyway?

You said the Word! Hankering, lusting, or pining for anything that is impermanent develops into an insatiable appetite—glut greed that can neither be quelled nor satisfied. An overpowering need which would eventually overpower your self. Those little creatures of greed wreak destruction with their tiny arms reaching far and wide, encircling and clasping in its firm grip, until you can no longer differentiate between your own self and those creatures. To lose its grasp over you, once it takes hold, requires the knowledge that such a hold is suffocating, snuffing your true potential and greatness that they eat into, like termites; leaving you hollow and empty with just a frame of a body! How would such knowledge descend on one who is surrounded by others who lust after that pygmy called greed? How indeed?

O little self, how are you going to combat this creature? And you talk about the good life? Know this—to crave for and lust after is to act under the directions of entities that create conditions, which you term as "effects." Are you willing to taste the conditions of such a need? If you say yes, to that I say, be prepared to face what you do not expect out of such a gain along with what you expect out of the same.

Those are the conditions you are now faced with, along with everyone who have so created such conditions. Some more will be the conditions, which you will again create through the ignorance of the senses. Think you that your spirit is so weak, so soft, and so mellow to require the cradle of a soft pillow? Look hard at this stuff you are made of. Look beyond your flesh and bones and noodle intestines. Look deeper than the red bulb of light that pulsates and throbs, that which you call your heart. This stuff that you are made of is as hard as the lustrous diamond. It does not require the pampering that your senses have created for you in a wimpy world, soft as a cushion rocking on a turbulent sea, never knowing when it is going to sink and clutching on to anything it sights; later deleting it from memory.

Material gain is for the soft and the vulnerable. For the impervious, the courageous and the indomitable, there are many more avenues to seek. Expectation in terms of material rewards does not guarantee you or anyone what you truly need or desire or what is expected of you. No god is soft and vulnerable, and you are all gods, every one of you. None of you on earth is spiritless. You have merely forgotten your powers. Forgotten who you truly are, and what it is that you are capable of. Once this is revealed, you would prostrate before your own self and before others in recognition of your reflection in them, and they in you.

O Soul, you have undoubtedly humbled me into asking many questions on relevant issues relevant to the world, as I know of. Yet I ask of you, pray, how does one live if one has a stomach to feed yet not seek monetary gain to feed that stomach?

How did you live before you created a monetary system, dear self? Did you not exist? Yes you did. But it was greed again that made you clash with one another, usurp territories that belonged to neither, yet belonged to everyone. You cheated and thieved and called it, "culture." You lied and deceived and called it, "civilization." You created coins and paper and gave it "value," and those became your true values. That became your god. But exist you must, and for the lack of a better knowledge, conceived a device whereby you could regulate the consequences out of the causes so conceptualized.

You created institutions to regulate the procedure of lying. You formed organizations to help apprehend those who lied worse than you but imprisoned those who lied less, in structures that you built as a form of reformatory retribution. This you called, "the calling of god." Then you conceived of the ultimate god force in the name of religion. This, you said, would show each and every one how to live a life (of lies) based on truth. Those institutions, which started off as a means to reach a goal, became an end in itself. You then appointed religious leaders who preached through an open mouth and a closed mind. These teachings you named, "morality."

Morality! How that very word makes me roar with laughter. But then again, how carefully you coined this word so as to have values to one group of people be termed as moral and to the others as immoral. That is the beauty of the wily mind that creates these concepts. And the suppression of sexual desires you call it as a gift to god? Can there be anything more hilarious? As if god wants to punish you for having been born with organs meant to perform what they perform. Who is this god, if not you and me? I do not want this gift. I experience love in its fullest, purest, form. When you and I both unite—that is my gift to myself.

This YOU, is your mind. Your ego, or external self, is the essence of the mind. Thus, mind and ego are one and the same. Your mind is represented by your ego. Which in itself is not bad. Ego has to exist otherwise I, your Soul cannot communicate to you. When we get connected and a communication link formed between you and me, then your mind is represented by your Soul.

Your mind is the essence of external experiences that your brain develops and collects. So too is the psychic being which develops in you and sometimes already exists in most of you. We shall deal with that later. For now, know that mind too is subtle like me. Your mind is thus the only part of you that can comprehend me and feel me and utilize me. Once it does this, its boundaries are widened and horizons expanded. But let not your mind take the driving seat. When I, your

Soul, guide the mind, your senses in turn are guided by the mind, and any action performed thus, is the highest form of creation. For I create. But reverse the order and it spells ultimate destruction. I tell you this—if you and all you gods, for gods you are, devalue that, which you value the most, there is no power attached to it. It is you that give power to any living or non-living being or thing. Without your power of valuation there is no value attached to anything. If you start valuing the words of your Soul to the price of your gold, the value of such words gains predominance. And when all of you commence your direction towards the attainment of your highest ideal, material gain takes a nosedive to the bottom most pits, like the plunge of stocks in a stock exchange market. These are the basic principles of valuation, a concept you have conceived.

In so giving importance to an external object you have created an entity with the power of such energy so thought of, for thought is energy and energy is thought. This entity so created rules you, or is ruled by you, until such a time when the ruler and the ruled, fuse with each other and become one. And this is what has happened with all of you and the material objects. You have mingled yourself and commingled with everything temporary so well that you have begun to reside in the object. The object now speaks for you, and hears for you. Your immortality reduced to life and death.

Consider an object beautiful, and you have given strength to that, rendering it beautiful. Consider it terrible, and it becomes so. What is this power? It is the same energy that pervades through the length and breadth of your being. A power so forceful that it either attracts or repels with intensity that you give it. With the same intensity do thoughts form. A feeling so passionate as to create and destroy as you "will." And when you bestow such passion on an animate or inanimate object of desire, a part of your power is depleted from you and delivered on to the object.

By giving thought to a thing called, God, the unseeable, you have created an entity with such thought and given it supremacy with your own fuel inside of you. Your fear of the same is you fearing your own strength, for you have given it the fuel to burn. The one constant factor in all of this is the power that is vested in you at all times. That which you call will, or Soul, subtle in its essence. In such a subtlety lies my energy. This is the energy that you possess. This is what you call, "God." This is the god that you are.

Alas! You just do not see it. For you insist on seeing it in the form of some physical entity. Woe is the musk deer that chases its own perfume knowing not the source of such an emanation, until it lies exhausted in a heap of ignorance. The same is the instance of an ignorant being, who unaware of his own spirit, condemns himself by succumbing to unnecessary trials and tribulations, of sufferings and despair, in search of glory, all the while the same lying within. For beings, are all of you, one and all.

Think you that you have come on earth to keep shop and play house? Do you devalue your Souls thus? The thunderous truth, however, will from time to time bellow out despite the torrential rains of suppression. The truth that is your Soul will remind each and every one of its presence until such a day when there is nowhere for you to hide. Truth is harsh and coarse to the mind fed by soft senses, like the cutting edge of diamond on satin. Come back again some other time should you find your soft little self too weak for me. Should the satin sheen hang limply and loosely on aged bones, like worn out drapes, come back to the hard luster of the diamond. For I Am the one with the rough edge which outlasts many a shine and sheen.

Yes, Yes, dear Soul, I have heard about this word "truth," several times, through several of my brethren. What is this truth? Is it the truth, which we speak through clenched teeth? Is it that truth that we, as politicians and administrators speak in closed rooms in oblong offices and oval offices through what we call, "open door policies?" Or is it that which lovers speak in clever, ambiguously wily and sly sentences, under the light of the deceitful moon?

Then we have the lawyers who admit a witness to the stand to make them speak the truth, the whole truth and nothing but the truth. Partial truth is not allowed in the courts of us truth-loving citizens. Of course the presiding judge sees only the truth and nothing but the truth yet the accused individual is not apprehended, after which, the lawyers, judges and several other witnesses write volumes on the truth of the case. The truth as they know it.

Many a time have I too spoken of what I perceived to be the truth, for I too, as a lawyer, had my witnesses swear to speak only the truth, to later realize that my truth differed from the others. The truth as I know it to be differs vastly from my neighbor's truth. Yet we all feel we are masters of truth. Thus we have several variations of one truth, and one version of several truths. All such truth in turn causing the others, me included endless pain.

The smoke in the room smote my eyes,
Heard I outside, the sound of lashing rain;
'Twas not the smoke, but the lies,
Which caused much sorrow, anguish and pain.
If there be beauty in truth,
And beauty is worshiped on Earth;
Why then do not people, the truth speak'st?
Or is there not meaning to the adage,
"Truth is beauty, and beauty truth?"

Which one of this is the truth, O knowledgeable one?

None my friend, none of what you know is the truth. So weep in silence if you must. For the truth has not as yet been received. Your whole world now lies in shambles. Tell this to your brethren and they will mock you and condemn you as a liar. For they wish to hear what they want to hear. Give them the truth and they will walk all over you like a herd of elephants. Utter the word, as it is, they will run you down. For those soft eyes cannot bear the brilliant dazzle of truth. Those delicate ears can only hear the clatter and jingle of coins.

Look at language that has been misused and abused; jingled and jangled, tangled and mangled. And you call it the language of the Soul? Seductive words encased in soft logic and a facade called reason; selective sentences with double-edged meaning lodged between reason and logic. Just like a philosopher lost in reason and the so-called practicalist lost in a sea of logic.

Value of truth is replaced by untruth based on fear factor. If the philosopher's philosophy and the Doctor's doctrine have an iron filing of truth in it, compulsion of seeing truth becomes irrelevant. Truth needs no compulsion. Truth needs no explanation or justification. That which justifies, or vindicates, or is compelled to explain, is not truth. Truth is fearless. It does not require the crutches and tools of explanations. Truth is invincible. The real world is trapped in an illusory world of falsehood—yet you speak of the truth! There is only one truth. Yet you talk of different individuals seeing truth in many different ways?

That is true, O great big self of mine. I have heard of the expression—"truth as is perceived...."

Perceived by what, O little ego? Perceptions based on messages sent by senses to the mind? Such truths will undoubtedly be many. Feel the truth with your Soul—through me. I always tell you the truth as it is, but you have ears only for the external. Then you have your mind vacillating like an oscillating pendulum between yes and no, clicking like a clock, to and from—back and forth. Finally you take the most convenient answer and deliver it as the voice of truth.

Oh no, dear Soul, we have no choice in choosing the truth, as we are given that truth by the mind after much thought and analysis. We analysts of finances and consultants of business, consult our mind before we utter any and every word. How then can you call them convenient? Truth does not come to us on a platter you know! We delve deep into our intellectual safes for the golden truth.

We are told by the authorities of knowledge that this darkness, of being unable to see the truth easily, is the result of the consequences created by the "Dark Age." We are also told that Utopia would automatically just emerge out of the blue and pull us out from this dark abyss. Thus, the cause of all this is the "Dark Age" and we have no control over it.

That's right, leave me in the dark recesses of your being and you will remain under such wraps and in perpetual darkness for the next hundred centuries. You and all of you render me shameful. I play no role. Mutely do I witness to all that is said in my name as the holy truth. Listen! Listen with all of your senses and your mind to what I have to say now. It is your instinct—your first action, unaided by external stimulus, which is the truth that speaks loud and clear. That instinct is my form of communication with you. For I am the force and my nature is action, at all times. I do not lie dormant in you. I pervade your entire being, sometimes getting into the mind and sometimes into and onto your senses. In and out, out and in, I undulate in total joy and abandon. But I can do this only when you open your mind to me. Then I communicate to you all the time at any time. A communication so subtle as to seem the workings of the mind.

How I long for such a communion. A communion of the external self, with me, the internal self. How I wait endlessly and tirelessly, for that light of illumination to glow in you and all of you. You walk about in the stealth of the night with the glow of high voltage lights, but of no avail such illumination to me. You still remain hidden in the dark, for you fail to glow from within. Fail to see the internal light that is me, shining harder than the fierce sun. You eclipse me with the dark moon of your ignorant thoughts. Yet I remain with a hope in my glow that you may some day see and shine as the luminous beings that you are.

2

If you chop wood, you have a fire.
But do it before the storm.
If you pick fruit, you have food.
But do it before it falls to the ground.
Remember to feed the tree that feeds you,
    else there will
be no fruit to eat or wood for a fire.
Take the light from your Soul.
But remember to nourish it, else there will
    be no light in the
Dark.

Glow, glow, as you go,
Brighter and lighter as uranium rays,
Bounce and fly, leap and flop,
Luminous, bulbous blobs of light,
In radiant circles of radium,
Bobbing up and down
In frenzied activity,
A mass of particles—unhomogenized,
From an electrocuted ego filled well called
humanity,
Into homogenized, conscious, non-recurring,
Eternal entities.

And what of action and reaction, O Soul? You mentioned something about external stimulus and instincts. What culminates in action and what leads to reaction? We are all action-oriented people. Look at the high voltage action we are involved in. We not only have action in the national and international arena; we have action in ordinary households too. Husbands taking action against the wife, wife taking action against such an action of the husband, by suing him. Yes, dear Soul, we love action. Are all these not action oriented?

Do not try to get frivolous with me, little self. Know this, as this is very crucial to your further evolution. Every motion or movement depends on action and reaction. Any act, performed under the guidance of the senses or external stimuli, results in a reaction. This is what you were talking about. What you called action is reaction. It is quite different from instinct, in that instincts always arise from the interior of a being. Instincts cause actions. The five senses that your body has are all external senses; therefore the energy that these senses are exposed to at all times causes them to react. Energy pervading in space, is the same within you. But that which is within you is a condensed, more self-contained form.

The one traveling in and around space is vast, non-contained and roaming indiscriminately everywhere, seeking similar patterns in individuals so it can link with the corresponding internal energy. Like a chain that has been derailed, it tries to magnetize another loop to link in its endless chain. The moment it detects the pull of an individual it draws and magnetizes it towards its vibrating pool.

Energy thrives on thought patterns and thought thrives on energy. When you charge your body with positive thoughts, you attract positively charged energy from outside, enhancing the inside of your luminous self that is me. Negatively charged bodies do not affect me in anyway. I do not cooperate with such an entity. Therefore, I grow less luminous to your overall self, as I slowly recede deeper under veils created by you. Your sensory nerves or external stimulus responds to any and every force it is so exposed to, rendering it vulnerable and totally under its sway, causing a condition of reaction. This in itself is neither good nor bad, except being useful or useless as the case may be.

Your instinctive response, which comes from within, from me, also acts through your mind and senses. But this is from inside out, therefore useful. The same cannot be said of the reaction of your nerves to external energy assimilated by your mind, which I consider as useless. Action and reaction are the basic differences amongst instinctive responses and responses from the stimulus.

When you will me into overpowering your mind into thinking on positive notes, deleting any whisper of unwanted thought lying in its crevices, then you empower yourself. And thus you have to empower yourself, for the time is nigh to manifest yourself in its true self.

But how am I to monitor my thoughts constantly, dear Soul? I have many times battled with petty trifling emotions taking over my most important thoughts, for I am a mere mortal. These trivialities take away most of my good thoughts. It is easy to say, but difficult to implement the process of thought monitoring. I have tried it, but my vanity comes in the way every time. Yes, I have many a failing. With so many emotional battles to fight, how am I going to sieve only those thoughts that are beneficial from those that are not? For thoughts do not come single file. They do not march in a disciplined manner. We order loving citizens leave such discipline to the armed forces. Thoughts come uncontrolled. Several of them occupying a single space in a fraction of a second like a crowded spaceless airplane.

That is the lazy mind dissuading you. Look, O fool, how cleverly it has manipulated you into thinking what is difficult and what is not. Did I not call it wily? Think you to be so weak as not to overpower it? It is not just your mind that is so crafty dear one; there are other entities called "ideas" floating around that enter into the area of dissuasion. At the right moment when your surging spirit gives an impetus to your highest goal, an incident or a distraction comes along, thwarting your plan for sometime.

A jealous strand of fiber strays into the vicinity hoping to steer you away from your highest ideal. You look at it and buckle under its deviously convincing skills. The essence of your will, which is your tool of applying me, your main will, which seemed uplifting one moment, suddenly deflates like a punctured balloon and you finally push it away locking it up forever—forgotten.

Conscious effort through me, your "will" or your "Soul" or your "self," all of this do I represent, eventually conquers the impossible. This is your ultimate conquest. To conquer thought with the help of your spirit or Soul or your will. Those thoughts, which you have gathered and harnessed over the years as a priori, or through prior knowledge, either through experiences or preconceived, ideas gathered from your senses, are an impediment to me. They create obstacles, as thoughts collected from such sources are not as subtle as the Soul's language.

Do you mean there are different types of languages? Is there one of yours and one that I talk in? I am confused dear Soul. What is this language? As it is we have different nations speaking different languages. We have a mother tongue and a father tongue too. Then we have one nation speaking several regional languages. And we have interpreters interpreting rightly or wrongly, as they choose to interpret. The rest of us take these interpretations as the actual word being spoken. Somewhere along the line, the true meaning of what is to be conveyed is lost in the melee of word traders.

Oh yes, we trade words too, for words mean money. Bombastic words, concise and precise words, a variety of words to suit every palate—we have invented all of this, for language is very dear to us. We attach importance to the nature of words, not to the feeling those words convey. Now you tell me that you too have a language. Which category does your language fall under, O knowledgeable one?

> *Image, dear one. Images and sublime feelings motivated by desire alone. That is my language. A desire which is creative. Which propels you forward into creating, without the condition of an expectation, without handing out a form with pre-drawn-out dictatorial terms. That which "does," and does not wait, for approval and rewards. Because it "knows." It is tranquil with the supreme knowledge of the motivator of such feelings. This is desire. Desire to realize myself in my ultimate form, which I call devotion. Any other feeling, is an emotion. I recede to the background in the absence of such a devotion and desire.*

You shine with the luminosity of love, yet know not of its existence. Love creates at all moments, every moment through thoughts evoked by you consciously. The creative use of thoughts is your inspiration, which leads you to faith in your "self," that is me. A faith so unshakable that even mountains tremble in submission at its intensity. A faith in the supreme knowledge of such a love as being god itself. A divine madness of self-intoxicating power, manifesting itself in every word uttered or action ensued from such a thought. A careless abandon enclosed in respect for the Soul—of the spirit defying death itself. For it is blissfully aware of its immortality.

How am I to know the messages from you, O Soul, and those that come from my mind? Confused and baffled I go around in circles and squares, from corners to the center and back to the corners. I am all the more confused when you use several names to call yourself. You call yourself, my Soul, my will, and my bigger "self," which one is the real you?

> *To answer the second part of your question—I am your Soul, the same that resides in every being. I am your will. I am your bigger "self." I am all this. Put your confusion on the back burner for a while and hear me out to the first part of your question. My messages always come from the feeling level. By feeling I do not mean emotions. Feelings are instincts. What you immediately feel to a given situation. This is quite different to reactions to external stimulus.*
>
> *Let me illustrate this with an example. Consider this, the sight of a man falling off a cliff or a tree or in some perilous danger; your instinct, that is me signaling, moves you into assisting the man without a thought for your own safety. Your mind on the other hand dissuades you, through reason and logic, into the safe keep of a prior knowledge. And in so doing, your own strength is underestimated.*

You deprive your Soul from exulting in its glory. The pinnacle of joy you exclude yourself from enjoying, through this selfish act. What is this joy? It is joy of overpowering fear.

The language of the Soul therefore, is only action. Seize this power from me and unleash me in my full manifestation. I am creation and creation alone. Destruction I know not of. I am the good that is in all and one, of evil I know not of. For all that is creative is good, all that is reactive I am oblivious to. To languish and suffer—a language of the body. I neither forgive nor wreak vengeance for I AM.

To you, O mind, I give these words that you may know what you are. You shall utter these words at all times in contemplation. To you I command, for you have to obey. That is the purpose of your creation, so you too may exult in ecstasy with divine passion and create. Dwell not on petty, trifling, fleeting distractions. O little self, that dances to the rhythm of the fleeting heart tell your wandering heart to squander not its affections on affectations. Steer it towards a love that withstands the harshest and severest storm that is I. Love me, your inner self, and you shall inherit the cup of elixir.

Hear then, my beloved exterior self, that which you shall utter when your mind is not engrossed in action of the Soul.

Thus shall you speak:

I am the creator,
I create out of nothingness,
I am perception and conception,
I perceive all there is,
I conceive and deliver
Bring to life out of void,
Giving it hues of multidimension.
I am the preserver,
I protect that, which I bring forth,
I am the giver and the taker,
This is my law of preservation;
I protect what is rightfully mine—my "self,"
The only thing which is whole.
I destroy in me,
Every idea of negation,
For I am the power and all there is,
Yet I constantly imbibe,
Every moment, something new and alive.
I am the all seeing and the all pervasive,
My power is within and without,
With which I feel.
I feel, therefore I am.

Your spirit or energy, O little self, does not exist to be utilized for remorse and repentance. It constantly moves up and down and everywhere. To repent is to pause. There is no cause to forgive, as I, your big Self—am forever, and remain untouched by those actions not directed through me. So grieve not on reactions committed out of ignorance. Replace it with continuous creation.

Now that we have that all cleared up, let me get on to my next most important question. We human beings talk of forgiving and forgetting a deed or a reaction, yet we do not forget. I can forgive yet I find it difficult to forget any incident. If a wrong were forgotten would it not be easy to repeat it again? Or is it that others wrongs should be forgotten and our own personal wrongs kept alive? Why this double standard? Should not one rule apply to everything and everyone? Please shed some light on this forgive and forget policy dear Soul, for it causes me much grief.

So many questions in one breath? Forgive what? What and who are to judge what is right and what is wrong? Think you to be the all knowing already to differentiate? Think again, and while doing so, remind yourself that you have to yet grasp knowledge in an ignorance-filled world. If you seek knowledge from the outside, then you have one right and several wrongs or, one wrong and several rights. Seek knowledge from the inside, that is me, and there is only an "is-ness" as is— the truth. Misgivings are musings of the mind. Since actions that require the use of such concepts are through the directions of the mind, outcomes ensuing from such actions are sorted out by the mind. Such reactions are the byproducts of emotions—emotions arising from the external senses directing the mind, hence non-productive.

Emotions like hate, fear and less realistic feelings are deviations from what I am. I only acknowledge love, which infuses everything you think of, touch and produce, with spirit, life and with energy. All that is not an affirmation is not the product of the Soul. Your very life itself is an affirmation of which you are. Then there are those that talk of renouncing life, to avoid the forgiving and forgetting policies that they created. They are in complete opposition to such an affirmation of life. There is no way of realization, save through collective consciousness. For am I not in all of your brethren? How then can you discard me, and selfishly seek a realization that brings no enlightenment to the collective self?

You seek forgiveness, what is there to forgive or forget? These words sound as hollow as the words spoken by moralistic preachers. Those Parrots, who mimic without "knowing." For who is greater or lesser than the other to impose on the other, virtues of the state? Who sits in judgement? Whose high throne sits on such a loose foundation? They are those who are ruled by emotions, and not by their Souls; those who are moved by reason and not by the passionate Soul, those who need to keep shop to maintain accounts like bookkeepers.

Ledgers and balance sheet of debits and credits, of good and bad, of right and wrong, they create. Studious and fastidious are they, in the give and take, with the policies they make. They create a heaven and hell too—these ledger makers. Heaven is for those who bear insults and injuries of the mighty, for "the meek inherit the earth," they chime, little knowing what it means. And hell is a cauldron of hot broth for those who harass the weak. The good get fewer and weaker by the hour—the evil get bigger and stronger by the second, "this is nature's laws of balances and bookkeeping," all of you say. "For the good to be realized, bad should exist," all of you judiciously nod your tremulous heads. "How else are we to know what is good, if we are not evil?" you justify.

Such, O dear one, are your principles of Nature's laws. All you wise individuals whose statements reek of indolence. You talk of forgiving? Seek forgiveness for those books you maintain with the assistance of your ever compliant, convenient mind. For they need to be preserved to remind humanity of how they demean themselves by being lesser than what they should in reality be. But alas! I cannot help but despair. Yes, I too despair at my own inability to make you see light through such a thick veil of darkness, like the smog that your vehicles emit. But such is the mind that is swayed by emotions. Emotions that belong to the territory of the senses alone. You have struggled with thought based on reason and logic as best as your senses could communicate to you. Love, as it should be—never experienced by your lesser self, and makes you fight with forces that should not be. The same forces that you term as good and evil.

So far you have not lived at all. You and every one of you do not live—you merely exist. For such an outwardly existence, you have laid all the trappings that the body can endure and not endure. Pined, lusted, and procured false ideals and goals. To maintain the charade of such ideals, you created good and evil. Of what use that goodness which recognizes evil? What is that evil which after being labeled as evil, continues to persist? In so recognizing evil, the good have honored evil to continue. The evil exonerated itself by condemning good. The cowardly ratified; thus gratifying the existence of both as a necessary evil, for the ultimate realization of an end that only spells annihilation of the final affirmation called life. Thus you sanction life.

Do I not have cause to despair? To despair, for not having lived at all. To mutely exist in a shell like a turtle, raising my voice every now and then, only to be squashed like a fly by the conniving mind. You immortal beings with mortal thoughts. Oh how you have thus insulted your own prowess! How you have tarnished the varnish of your being! Yet you dare to talk of redemption? You hypocrites of the Soul! You cowards who dare not look deeper into your own selves for the fear of losing your shell of ignorance. Does knowledge so frighten you? Is ignorance truly bliss to you? Then why do you pray with frightened minds and a shuddering body?

This is what your prayer sounds like to me:
Dear god—forgive us for our pretenses,
As we forgive those who pretend to us—
As I pretend to you—
So they to me,
Thus and only thus can we keep the circle
of
ignorance recurring,
To continue on in desperation,

With beads of toil and perspiration,
We lead each other in a rigmarole—
That our senses lead us into,
As we "allow" it to lead us into,
A world of make believe and pretensions,
For we know not the power of reality,
Of fear and cowardice our hearts fill,
And rent the air with false promises,
Of hope and love—joy and bliss;
While, with one eye open, we furtively avoid our
unfailing friend—Death,
The other we slyly open to the mind of greed,
Yet we beseechingly seek,
The kingdom above, while we know it is within.
Groping and floundering in this endless abyss,
We look for that garden called happiness;
So bless us all, while we wantonly continue,
In our self destructive garden called "ignorance,"
And thus we wait for a torch of light—in the guise of a messenger,
Which we promise to promptly extinguish, before the
Rooster can thrice crow,
So we can in unison once again; petition our redresses,
Seeking your forgiveness and deliverance,
In order to complete the wheel of life and death,
And blame it on cause and effect,
If not, how can we justify our means?

The end to us—irrelevant.
The whining, whimpering business man—
The pathetic sympathy seeker, looking for
a grain
of compassion,
So when the need arises, we as charity
creators—deign
to help,
Fulfilling yet another of our many
pretensions.
The artist, the poet and the musician,
Singing lyrically—rhymeless themes and
rhythmless tunes,
In off key voices—in tremulous treble
That bounce off deaf walls and empty
rooms.
The Pope, the priests and humbug
divisions,
Enveloped—entrenched in a fanatical
world,
Under the guise of morality.
But hark!—There is a thunderous applause,
We applaud ourselves for an act well
performed,
For is not the world a prancing stage?
Where we are all told to masquerade,
As fooling Toms and Tomfoolery?
With tin cans rattling as heads, we preen
and peer,
At empty reflections—shallow self (less) self
(ish) entities;
Paint smeared on faces of guile,
Pretending, masquerading all the while,
To our own selves; a fool of which,
Hast our senses made of us, we admit;
But are too cowardly to admit our failings,

For the fear of hurting our ego.
So deliver us from our own self inflicted
miseries,
For we love to blame our conditions,
On that first cause called creation.

Consider me cruel; consider me benevolent, it matters not what you further accuse me of. But I shall persist until the rest of you realize and release yourselves from the soft blanket of luxurious words, which lull you into a sleep of ignorance. Harsh these rebukes sound to you, yet not a grain of deceit in them. Deny this and you deny truth.

3

It is easier said than done, there is no denying that. But once said, hear it from the preacher and implement it. In so doing, the reap of the harvest is more than the seed of the preaching.

When the mind is fettered by thoughts
of mundane existence,
Means of livelihood take new dimensions,
Effect precedes the cause,
Origin and beginning is on pause;
Love recedes and emotion succeeds,
Secondary, subsequent illusion supersedes,
That which is passion,
Remains a notion.
Lust over sanity,
Superficiality and vanity,
Overlays reality,
Blinding, confusing, humanity—so chaotic,
Rendering that which is, as was,
That which never was, as is,
If this is not an illusion, then what is?
For reality unwittingly shoved into an
abyss.
Mass floundering with flaying arms,
Led by the blind and the mute into an
unending,
A tunnel of darkness,
A vacuum of despair,
All the while pretending;
Practicing and preaching,
The truth as can be seen,
For it never has been,
While the poor Soul inside,
Mute witness to the outside,
Waiting to be heard, to be recognized,
It's true self to be realized,
Not by the "lone,"
That remains few and far between.
And so it sighs, lamenting,
"Break free from this bondage,
Unfetter the chains that so suffocate;

Neither man nor child as yet know'th,
The freedom that remains elusive,
To the oppressive and the submissive,
For freedom is neither oppression,
Nor is it submission,
But it is action,
The ultimate self realization,
Of changing the old order,
To the golden and the new,
Of the paradise that was never lost,
As it never was sought.
Awake and arise the slumbering 'me'
Let the flame of passion ignite,
From me to you,
And you and you,
Until each and everyone with hands raised,
Hearts linked and Souls entwined,
Ascend space, transcend time.
The above, the below,
The here and the beyond,
All rolled into one and one into all,
O vain thought, do hear my call,
Unwind from the dreary mundane,
To the vastness, the gigantic that is the real you,
The deepness and the nothingness
Yet everything-ness,
Come then reclaim that, which is your sanity,
Unto such time will time exist,
Unto such an eventuality will space conceal,
The inner dimensions to the outer dimensions."

You have wanted the truth—you shall have it! This is the cost of such knowledge. That you pay the price of admitting and acknowledging conditions, the way they are. That you pave the way and path for those still under wraps of illusions. That you render each word as is said, without encasing it in words with frills and finery—which you call tact and diplomacy. For truth requires no lame assistance.

The appalling gloom of desperation you have caused to exist; the destitute conditions that other individuals experience are all your creations. Such conditions have no right to exist. You are the creator of the Universe, and have forgotten to remember this. You are a blob of energy, with energy fields around you on which you thrive. To utilize these force fields you have to comprehend the magnitude of such a force and consciously apply them. This little detail has slipped your mind. Not because of any preconceived devious plan that you call, "a grand design," but the inability of energy to manifest itself, save through the physical matter.

To realize this, you have already done the preparatory work, but cannot see beyond the conditions you have created for yourselves. These conditions which you call "effect," is consuming all of your energy.

But how can what is done be undone, O great self? Is this not the way it is meant to be? What of destiny and fate, and the reasoning of "things the way it is, to serve a purpose," are they not good enough reasons for the prevalent conditions?

Yes, my little self, crawl back into that moth infested riddle, which you call life. Tremble like an ancient philosopher and seek shelter in such ambiguities. Go back and run helter-skelter, run amuck to those dogmas of the eternal ring of recurrence. For that is what you wish. You do not seek to be immortal. You cry for the putrid stench of burning flesh of convenience; not for the nectar of elixir. What know you, of the bliss of nectar, you thieves who steal the nectar of the bees? That is your power is it not? Your right of "puny might." You run for miles in fear of the sting of those very bees you steal from!

You hide in the moonlight to war with the sun. And you call yourselves warriors? You call yourselves brave and wage wars for lustful gratification! And you ploy and toy with phrases like "war being a necessary evil." Yes, my friend, go back to the comforting arms of destiny. What know you of power? You leeches and parasites, calling yourselves paragons of virtue. Your thoughts are as frail as your frames. You sing the same listless, mournful tunes you call Soulful. Fate and destiny you say, "man is powerless against." "Time," you say, "is the best healer," and wait. "Space," you say, "is infinity and thus beyond our reaches." You wait for death in order to go to what you call, a "heaven." So you sit waiting your entire lives that you call, "lives of piety." Waiting for a golden invisible vehicle to lift you body and

Soul to another realm. Your lazy bodies have rendered your mind lazy with the words of destiny and fate.

You call yourselves, inheritors of the earth? You are nothing but mere borrowers, borrowing and lending, lending and borrowing to continue on with your petty trade. You borrow time to extend life, borrow space and deplete its layers, borrow earth and evade payment. Truly you are store managers, bargaining for a few extra morsels. What of rhythm and rhyme, tune and song? Did you not borrow these too from the cuckoo and the nightingale? And then you mercilessly imitate it, mimic it while it so poignantly and valiantly sings its tune. What is that which is truly yours that you cling on desperately to your borrowed material?

With such truth lying naked as a bald eagle, you feign ignorance and deafness. All you can hear is your mind shrieking—'mine, mine.' Which is why you have gone deaf and mute. How can you catch the gentle whisper of messages carried by the breeze, when you can only hear your mind bellowing? How can you see other forms in space, when your mind sees only that which glitters? Like the crow that pounces on glittering objects, so you run after all that glitters.

O Soul, many a time have I wondered about the secret behind what we term as "happenings." Many a moment have I attributed an event to "chance." Now you say, there is no destiny. How am I to understand why certain occurrences render themselves as unavoidable accidents, or chance happenings? Will I ever learn how to avert an accident or refrain from entering an area where damage control is minimum? I seem to be running into several such "chances," only to have my fingers burnt each time. I later pacify and console myself with such words as "destiny," as this is what I find solace in.

Hear me now, O little self. Hear me with the ring of eternal truth. Hear me as distinct as the loudest bell that you can produce. Destiny and fate are words—mere words. They have no feeling. Those words, which have no feeling, are not messages from me. All my images have words, and all word images. Show me if you can an image for destiny. Can you feel destiny? What you cannot feel, does not exist. What you call chance, or accidents, are incidents which have a life form of their own. A life form that you create with your own thoughts, unconsciously. Conscious living thus becomes imperative if you wish to understand how to use the energy fields around you.

You are an orb of light radiating and emitting currents, waves of emanations, from your entire being. Any thought, thought of, immediately acquires energy. Thus you build little pockets of energy. The more intense your thoughts, the greater the velocity of these pockets. Emanations arising from you find similar emanations in the surrounding atmosphere and vibrate to the tune of the same, like a chorus song. What happens next is, you have created an event for which you had no conscious idea of, or had no physical effort put into the same. This is what you term as "chance."

Accidents occur in a similar manner. An atmosphere charged with tension, charged with thoughts of individuals surrounding you and your own, intermingle with one another through emanations produced by you and those around you. They find compatibility with similar vibrations in the outside atmosphere and form a boulder like energy of negatively charged currents. Thus without any pre- warning an accident occurs in your surrounding area. If you were to consciously utilize your thought process, you could either avoid the same, or release positively charged emanations from your being and completely changes the scenario.

Imagine, if you will, a basketball court or a football stadium packed with people having various thought processes cheering either of the group players or neither, they thus charge the field with their emanations. If you happen to be a player with mixed feelings about the result of the match, you create a "doubt boulder" around you and immediately become susceptible to similar emanations in the atmosphere. You become the target. How does this happen? Those emanations find a similar set of waves with your negatively charged vibrations, and thus find an entrance into the bubble of emanations you release from your being. If on the other hand you remain conscious of your thoughts, and allow only those thoughts to enter your mind which assure you of success the game is yours.

But would it not be possible for me to wish harm on another by utilizing such forces negatively? What if I have access to such energy manipulation, and I possess negative intentions? Would that then not cause grief to another individual? And what if the mass population went around utilizing energy for individualistic purposes? Good God! I dread to think of the result.

And that is what all of you have been doing to each other consciously or unconsciously. Some of you had access to enormous powers. I talk of an age when man knew what it was to be god. Jealousy and greed overpowered their minds. Minds took shape as entities that controlled such beings. Eventually, over the years man forgot that he once possessed such powers. When the mind begins to act as a separate entity from the Soul, it loses contact with reality—the reality of the Soul. Once such a contact is lost, your powers elude you. Your powers are meant for greater things than for the use of petty, paltry musings of shop keeping and window-shopping. Synthesis of energy arising out of your "being," and those emanations from the outside of your being, merge into each other producing an invisible entity. This entity is your very own creation. Reversal of thought or the deletion of such thought that created this entity does destruction of the same. These emanations are so subtle; the visibility of which is rendered impossible to the naked eye. Especially to that eye which is so habituated to seeing only what it wants to see.

Are you curious as to what these entities do? They carry out your orders. Yes, they are obeying entities, for are you not god? Are you not the creator of their existence? Unaware to your own external self, you create invisible entities. Entities that surround you like moths to a flame. They metamorphose into independent, invisible beings like a caterpillar into a butterfly, and circulate in the atmosphere, which you can recall at any given moment. These are the good and evil forces you originate through your very own emanations. When you obey them they become evil entities, for they control you. When you command them, they behave in accordance to you. Thoughts diffuse pure energy from inside you and form finished products and send them into space.

This is your very own satellite space ship that you send out. Such a product is an entity. Sometimes two or more individuals, who emanate the same thought or somewhat similar thought, diffuse the exact quantity of energy into the atmosphere. Such entities find each other in the open space, fuse into one big boulder like formation, and hurl itself into infinite space picking up similar energy diffused elsewhere. What is in you, is out there too—the useless and the useful energy. Whenever any being strikes up a thought that is similar, that being taps into this boulder, which acts as a store house of tiny fiber like current waves. This is how one thought rolls into the other, fusing and diffusing and then dispersing, with no first or last thought, no beginning or end. They spin through space in concentric circles in a circular motion. Whenever it finds a being thinking about it, it rushes into the vicinity of that being. Thus you may find two people thinking about the same idea at the same time. It just means, both of them have tapped into the same energy-boulder.

The same holds true for energy created by thoughts of greed, vengeance and every other subsidiary feeling called emotion. You create as many entities as the number of thoughts that you think of and dwell on. But these energy forms are clothed in a subtle substance, subtler than space. With eyes and ears trained to see and hear material substance, subtlety is lost on you. You talk of recurrence—there are no recurrences, only occurrences. You cause it to occur or to disappear. No ledger keeper has maintained your records to organize and plan a life for you here on earth. You have not come with any purpose, but seek a purpose to justify your existence.

Now that you exist, your goal, unknown to you, is that of physical immortality. Is that not what all of you want? Eternal life, eternal youth! To want it and to desire it is not a sin, as your moral preachers have told you. There is no sin save that of non-action. Your secret longing for eternity. That yearning which you suppress so cleverly and keep. I know it. For I long for you to be eternal. In your eternal life is my mission completed.

4

Knowledge not applied is
like a clouded sun in orbit.

But the conditions have already been created. What is done, cannot be reversed. And the done causes some more effects, thereby creating more consequences out of a previous cause. Thus we go chasing the effects of a previous cause, and the effect thereafter becomes another cause for the following effect. It seems to be a vicious cycle, never ending and all consuming. All-consuming because all our energy is expended in theorizing and analyzing about and around the cause and its effect. How can we undo conditions created by hatred and jealousies?

I am not above such jealousies either, O Soul. I cannot seem to rise above such pettiness although much effort is spent on overcoming the same. How does one not allow jealousy to creep in? It comes very naturally to us, as easily as the air we breathe. And hatred? Flames of hatred, which we make no effort in dousing, engulf us all. Not because we do not want to, but because we do not know how to. What started off as smoke turned out into forest fires, and now the leaping flames of hatred have begun blowing international clouds overhead. How is one to overcome something of such a magnitude?

> *You overcome jealousies by running your own race, at your own pace. Adopt this attitude and conditions evaporate as steam. By concentrating on your action without glancing at another person's action or reaction, you build energy forms of a positive nature. Every filament and fragment of such a form negates ten times the amount of negative energy caused by those individuals who create energy forms with their reactions. When you take cognizance of the circumstances, you deviate from your target. Every being is great, every being is small. None is greater*

than the other is or smaller than the other. Competition arises from a need. Need of what? Is not the entire world yours? Is not the achievement of one individual, yours too? You, however, have your own lane to run on. Peering over your shoulder to glimpse at the other runners distracts the attention so required by you for the achievement of your goal. Contentment that you too are god, should be your attitude at all times. This is the key to your success in evolving as a being. For that is man's ultimate goal, to become into a being. The routes taken by each may differ; the goal remains the same. What is already done, can be undone by not taking the done into cognizance. When you acknowledge that hatred exists, you give it value. Thus its importance increases.

Hatred knows when and where to strike. When it spots the energy of an individual waning, it sees it as a signal to enter into the external energy space of the said individual. It therefore comes within the vicinity of the concerned individual, who reacts to it. This reaction is the act of the senses and the mind, and not the Soul. Thus, your first reactive response to such an external stimuli, should be questioned, cautioned and quieted. By so doing, you allow for the opportunity of your will or Soul prevailing upon you. Your best and highest attitude toward conditions created out of hatred would be, to devalue it by disclaiming its existence and continue with your constructive actions. Just as one ignores the tantrums of a child. This is the only way you surround your self with a film of positive ions, which acts as an impenetrable fortress.

Consciously, with the very fiber of your being, that is me, involve your self in action and refrain from reactions. Ignore the conditions already in effect. Thus you obliterate its very existence. Heed not to compelling voices of destruction, for they can be very seductive. Adhere not to the external urges of retaliation, for they are mischievous in their intentions. Counsel with the group of lawyers residing in you, with the judge at the helm of affairs, that is me.

Similar to hatred and envy, is pleasure and pain. The pleasure pain principle does exist, when it has no right to exist. They are irrelevant sensations to me as energy. But to you as feeling, living, breathing individuals, they are part of the bodily sensations. They affect you, and so they affect me. To be oblivious to pain and pleasure and pretend they do not exist, or to dismiss them as illusions, is hypocrisy. To admit they exist, and say, "I suffer, but I have a goal to complete," are words of the courageous. "I revel in pleasure, but I have a mission to accomplish," are words of the truthful. "This is the way life is meant to be," are words of the cowardly. For pleasure and pain need not exist. You are to overpower in order to evolve from the pain and suffering principle. In such an overpowering, you start the process of "becoming."

The old order has to give way to new. When the old becomes obsolete and immaterial to the process of evolution, it gives rise to new. For evolve you must. Your evolution from energy to life, from life to mind and mind to consciousness and super consciousness is the final goal.

Your religious dogmas propound and dictate their doctrines that have gone obsolete with time, convincing humanity all the while, into an existence of resignation, thus impeding and obstructing human evolution. They teach and preach about accepting things as they are as "a plan of god,"—does not your spirit rise in indignation at this untruth? Do you not feel me turn inside of you when you utter such false convictions? Have the philosophers' spirit gone weary of carrying their tedious yoke of wisdom? Why such destitution of your Soul? Do I not shout the words of truth loud enough for the entire world to wince under such veiling of the truth?

Why, O ignorant one, do you ward me off from revealing myself? The utterance of words such as, "pain and suffering as a necessity" is like milk gone sour. Rise from such resignation. Suffering is not deliverance. It is unnecessary. Why do you still suffer? As long as you do not accept that you are god, you will continue in ignorance. As long as you veil the truth with your convenient lies, shall you wallow in self-pity at your plight. Only that is veiled which is one of shame. Are you so ashamed of yourself? Why the guilt and the shame? Shake the veil off such idiosyncrasies. Your suffering pains me and causes me much anguish and sorrow. Oh how I do love thee, yet thou dost not love thyself! Thou think'st thou art alone when thou can'st share thy grief with me.

The cloaks of illusion created by superfluous concepts are the products of connivance, which you call intelligence. For the fearless and the undaunted, such mendacious concepts are revealed. The cowardly and the superficial hide beneath the veneer of the middle road stance they undertake, of the principle of pleasure and pain as necessary elements. How then are you going to overpower my little ego? Are you well equipped to battle with them? Are you a warrior resplendent with all the virtues required of a fighter? Or do you waste your effulgence on petty bickering and quarrels of territorial supremacy, like leeches? I say this to you; there is no other power worthy of pursuing than the power of the spirit. To squander your thoughts on stripping each other bare of the material, increases your infliction of pain on yourself along with all others. Empower your mind and suffuse it with my energy. Give your mind some work to do. Let it know that you have a commander and it is not "it." Allow me to pervade your entire mind, leaving no space for its independent thought and action. Let me uproot the rotting, decaying pain, and choke suffering even before it gurgles likes a stuffed up nozzle. For I believe in an eternal human power being the supreme power—the Supreme Being. For I love you, O mind.

I too long for a release from this bondage of suffering that I silently bear. Of being bound inside of you with no outlet. Fervently I keep hoping time and again, to be able to fully enjoy that which I created. And before I can begin to breathe the beauty of my creation, you snuff out your life by inviting death, like those candles you burn and snuff out.

Ah, my little self, are you so ashamed and embarrassed to live a life of plenitude? Why do you torture yourself thus when I promise you bliss and ecstasy? But the time has come when no amount of your refusal will hold sway over that which is already in progress; the overpowering of your mind by a more subtler being. I shall invade all thoughts to shatter the image of ignorance created by the ignoble mind. No more entreaties and pleas. For long you have basked in ignorant delight. Now you shall live in enlightened bliss—eternally. Of a mind which will think of little else than the creative powers. Of thoughts created by a subtle mind. Of imaginations which will breathe the fresh air of noble spirits and not the decomposing odor of degeneration. Such will be the magnitude of my lightning rod, which I shall strike and charge the atmosphere with.

Great Soul that would mean control by you and god does not control. It, or she/he, allows chaos to run amuck so nature can take care of itself. This, we humble individuals know as natural laws that god created for us to exist and we meekly take.

Such are the words of the irresponsible. To take responsibility for one's actions and be the god you are would mean too much of work would it not? For your sloth filled slovenly selves would like to wreak the havoc you are wreaking yet blame another fictitious entity that you have created.

God you say does not control? It controls. You are god and you control only that which you want to. Know that it is your power that controls your senses. You call this, self-control. You say, "an appetite not controlled leads to disquiet." And so you control an aspect of life you want to control. Yet you conveniently disallow your mind to be subjected to the control of your Soul. When the state of conditions of your conception gets beyond your mental and physical capabilities, you look upward for your ultimate savior. A visible manifestation of an invisible being to set right what you think is wrong, only to resort to the same tricks once again, as a failure student repeating the same class over and over.

Where does this power come from do you think? From your mind you assume. "Mind over matter," you say. Thus you would like to limit your glory to the mind alone, in total disregard to the super mind that is me. "The root of all unseemly desires is vested in the mind," you lament. You reproach yourself for not having enough self-control over your senses, yet you continue. You continue because you want to.

Where there is a will there is a want, and where a want, a will. A want which is of a nature suitable to the will. A want which would enable the will to control reactions. A want that wills action. This is the want, which is the final affirmation of life. But then, what know you of such an affirmation you negators who negate life? Your affirmations reek of stale thoughts like the air in a closed room. Those thoughts are where it is supposed to be, enclosed in that which you guardedly enclose it in; in archaic records. Thoughts comatosed into concise, dispassionate words, in neat columns of systematic entries. Entries of error in ledgers and account books, labeled Reason, Logic—Expectations. An account of a barter system you have perfected. You call this, intelligence. It is precisely this intelligence which controls you. An intelligence with which each individual tries to outdo the other with. You call this super intelligence and the pioneers of the same are the intellectuals of the shallow society you create.

Those who see not such intelligence are not worthy of a life, therefore deserve to be reduced to sub-human lives, you feel. "God is unfair" you lament—"he bestows intelligence to some and none to the others." So you wallow in self-pity. Now your ledger books have rotted and you detect an error in them. "Equality and inequality, are the creations of Nature," you cry out. "Oh how helpless are we, for we are but human and to err is human." Thus you console yourselves. But you know not, that you are a human with super human powers. Your exterior misleads you and places you in a hapless condition. Break free from such boundaries and think with the will of your super powers inside of you. The dimensions of your will far exceed those of your wants. Travel on the beam of your will and inequalities mitigate itself. Listen! Listen to your heartbeat! Does it not beat with the rhythm of every living being on earth? Your beat pulsates with the beat of every other, the resonance of which is the dance of life. How then can anything be considered unequal and equal? How can Nature beat another drum elsewhere? Is it not you who have created such a condition through your base lust for power of a lesser thing?

Men have made women weak by demeaning their physical prowess and women have, secretly with their hearts desire, made men impotent. Both jointly have designated animals and insects and every crawling creature, as objects meant for their consumption. "For, is not the earth and its uses meant to be pillaged and looted?" you innocently conclude. Treasures of the earth— you, and every one of you are such treasures too; lamentably plundered and misused. Your booty you claim, nay, you snatch, gorge and gormandize much beyond your appetite. You suffer from indigestion that your glut causes. Your insatiable needs make you dig deeper into earth for more of its treasures in total oblivion to the existing factors of the grains of sand being depleted; crushed by menacing arms of greed.

Think you these are "wants?" They are the worms inside of you that crave for your ultimate destruction. Time is nigh that the forces will control instead of you controlling it. This is your ultimate annihilation. Is this how you want your ignorance to be annihilated? Woe to all the annihilators of such power.

But I shun and mock at such. I, who am the ultimate "will," shall reverse such a trend. I, who am the preserver of life, reject your desire of annihilation. I, as the creator, shall preserve by a mere skein of thought. For I balance the entire universe and all such universes with the power of thought.

5

When one thought by one individual coincides with another, the energy that such thought emits find compatibility with each other, therefore the connection of two or more like-minds.

With passions flared,
Wild flames beyond compare,
Bursting, fuming, engulfing, ensnaring,
Spreading its arms flaying,
Like thoughts screaming inside the head.
Hot lava erupting from volcanoes red,
The fury of gushing streams,
Flooding fields of corn that sweeps,
O'er mighty gigantic terrain,
On slopes and hills and unknown valleys;
But then a benign light o'er and above,
Nowhere, somewhere yet everywhere,
Beneath, within and without, now and forever.
An infinite row of bright hue
Of pattern-less mass, now stopping, now
flowing,
Each aglow in beatitude, yet not knowing,
Until the patterns together as one,
With the corn, the streams and the gathered sun,
Journey inward, in the somewhere, nowhere and
everywhere,
Alongside the outside and the inside—towards,
Adorned with passion benign,
The fury, the glory, the ultimate and the sublime,
That which is goodness, as in you so in me.

O Soul, you have said time and again about the power of thought. What is this power? Is every thought powerful? What is thought, and how does it acquire power? All that we are aware of is only the material power. And this includes physical power too. Power, as we mortals know, is the fear and awe instilled in those who do not have it by those who have it. The use and abuse of power! This is what power does. Yet you talk of power in such glowing terms? And what of the power of us women who feel powerless in a man's world? What of that power that makes men feel disrobed by the women? Oh yes, with all the power we still remain powerless in the face of power. A mightier power makes us less powerful, and hence inadequate and therefore the various insecurities and psychological problems we are faced with.

Man, woman and child, without any distinction, possess insecurities of one kind or several kinds. None of us are without such feelings. These insecurities lead to jealousies, which eventually turns to hatred, an emotion so strong its effect is ten times more devastating than an atom bomb. Yet you talk of power? Of what use this power that some feel threatened by, most feel insecure without, and many do not know what to do with it? Pray enlighten this humble woman, dear Soul.

Power as you know is not the power I speak of. Power that is magnificent, power that is invincible, and such is the magnitude of power. This is the power of thought. Let me explain to you, O dear one, for you seem to be in a state of perpetual confusion. Thought is the feeling of desire created by the energy you call as spirit.

Energy with positive and negatively charged particles surge throughout the length and breadth of your body and mind. Thought is powerful because it is charged with energy, which it disperses outside of the self, as soon as a thought takes shape. Where do these thoughts come from? You might question. They originate from the exterior and from the interior.

So thoughts and the energy that such thoughts contain, exists outside of our individual heads too?

Hear me out first. Those thoughts originating from the exterior are perceptions developed through the five senses, internalized over the years as remembrances, which may be recalled at will. Thoughts originating from the interior of your self, are the actual thoughts, as they emanate from the feeling level, straight from the conscious. The more intense your level of feeling, the more intense and powerful is your thought, and more energy is utilized towards the creation of such a thought. But here is the key to the lock of your boundless spirit. Any feeling that is associated with action produce thought, which replenishes your energy spent on it.

Those feelings (that you term negative) which are reactive in nature, eat into your energy supply depleting it. Intensified, reaction takes on enormous proportion of destruction as opposed to construction. Thus thought, active and reactive has the power of manifesting physically in the material world. This is power. The power of thought emanating from within. Power that empowers you with a feeling of invincibility. This is achieved only by thought. Your lamentations of power of men and women are baseless, for no other power can be called POWER, except that of the mightiest thought.

Your thoughts of inadequacies are baseless. Whine not to me, for you will not get any sympathy. It is the sympathy seeking habit that strips you and diminishes your power. Women have all the power, yet they know not that they have it. Men have all the power yet they look outward for the same. Each and every thought, thought of has been thought before, in a different shape and form. That, which you call "knowledge," exists on its own, waiting to be discovered. You just happen to discover it. When mind starts to think, it does not necessarily use all other sensory organs to assist it. Your previous association with a certain smell or color or taste or touch gives you certain ideas, which the brain stores in itself. Other information received through other sources is also stored in the brain. When the mind taps into energy fields outside of the body, it could be positive or negative, depending upon the mind's desire to create or destroy. If it is a creative idea, you tap into positive energy. This energy is an emission from various other individuals, living and dead. The energy so emitted is not necessarily a raw form, but most of the time, one that has been turned into a finished product, waiting for another entity to help in its physical manifestation.

The same is that of negative energy floating and flitting in the atmosphere. Tap into it with the negatively charged thoughts that you emit and, boom!—Physical materialization of the very thought takes shape, right before your eyes, much to your astonishment. The energy, which is within the body, is the same as that existing outside. Thus if you utilize your energy, and combine the outside positive energy and shape it to a desired form, the result is an outstanding manifestation of the purest thought. Therefore, if the mind were always employed in thoughts, which are useful, it would not be too difficult for it to consequently perform acts, which you would normally term as miracles. Any thought or idea, which negates the affirmation of life, is an impure thought. Every thought, which is an affirmation, is a pure thought. The affirmation is—I Am creation. Negation is—I Am destruction. Feelings that arise from me are all such affirmations. Thoughts that arise out of such feelings are always those that involve action.

Thought-Attitude-Action. Action, Attitude, Thought. Whichever way you reverse this triangle, it feeds itself and increases its dimensions proportionately, in accordance to the level of intensity. Thought leads to the projection of your outward person into and onto the universe. Such an attitude is not just effective on the everyday people you meet and communicate with, but with the entire universe. Plant life, animal life, space and the unseen energy; each of these, together and separately are affected by your thought and attitude. Attitude leads to action, which again leads to thought with an increased or a decreased level of energy, depending upon the nature of such a thought, thought of. Thus the cycle continues, like a ball set in motion, gathering skeins and pieces of similar energy that it gets attracted to on its journey. This ball that you propel into motion comes back to you again, picks up its antenna for more messages and sets rolling once again. Self-feeding it may appear, but its source is you and you alone. Which is why the necessity of cultivating mind becomes necessary. Just as you cultivate every stance and nuance, your voice and gait, (which is not that important) so too shall you mold mind to the dictates of your will.

"Where do you play a role in all of this energy building and thought developing project, dear Soul? Looks like you have left all the work to me. And you are very harsh too. I need some warmth from your words, dear Soul. The warm sun, the warmth of human bodies and warm red wine that warms the heart, is not sufficient. My senses need to be constantly pampered to be able to get to work. All my brethren and me yearn for soft words as opposed to severe ones, as they are more pleasing and easy to wash down. Please, Oh please, I beg you, do be soft with your whiplash of words. This sensitive skin cannot endure any more heat. Enough has it endured already.

You protest too much, just as much as your protestations against your institutions that you have created. You create and yet you protest? You and all of you have built these words that you call language, and yet you find it hard to digest? Why create them when it is unpalatable? If I tell you how much I love you, my dear ego, would that make you warm and happy? Would that make you lazy and indolent as you have thus been? Would that procure any result from you other than slouch on the couch?

No, my dear little self, twice no! I shall continue with this barrage of words until you rise and act. You are not alone in the energy building project, as you call it. I am with you all the time. You just do not feel me. I am as subtle as the air you breathe. To feel me, your mind and your body have to acquire the state of subtlety. I am the manager of your energy. When I am involved in the management of your energy, I always exude power and employ you in useful (not gainful) application of such energy. I remain the silent witness that I am, unless you approach me. With vanity discarded, I, the egoless self, become accessible to you. But just as soon as a streak of the superficial is detected, I disappear back into my shell.

And why this game of hide and seek? I am tired already and I do not wish to play peek-a-boo. Could you not just appear, and put us all out of this endless game of discovery and self-discovery? As it is we have endless avenues to discover to now have to undergo another voyage into ourselves to discover our "self."

Alas! That is my deficiency and there lies the discrepancy in creation. Would you be satisfied if I apologized to you right now at my inability? My inability to surface out in the open in any and every condition, is a flaw that you have to assist me with to overcome. I am not perfect as you think me to be. Had I been the master of perfection, could I not have as easily realized myself, without putt-

ing you through an endless maze of self-discovery and voyages into the interiors of your Soul? Your spaceships traverse the skies, which makes it accessible to you, yet I remain elusive to you.

How deep is my agony for such an unapproachable role that I play, you know not. For I too yearn for that all-tempting elixir of eternity. With such a fond hope I make you dream of fantasies, which is as a matter of fact, a reality. A reality that remains a fantasy as long as it cannot be discovered. With such a hope, I cause you to strive endlessly and ceaselessly so you may taste the bliss of eternal life. I am the raw unfinished product with intelligence and power, but you are the physical manifestation of which I am proud. You make me glow internally, yet you allow not the glow to live forever. Yes, my innermost desire is for a physical life that does not perish, suffer or wither. Thus I leave this task unto you. In this lies your greatness, and my greatness reflected in you. We are both invincible, you and I. Have I not said that time and again? This is what you need to do, to accomplish this task. Follow the route of every feeling and thought and more importantly, never give up your highest ideal. Never give up your highest dream. Never relinquish your highest goal. Let your mind, during its break time; dwell on those magic words of your goal.

How high can your mind climb the ladder of thoughts, my dear little self? Will it stop at the base rung of the ladder of barter and exchange or can it go to its highest peak without a fall? For fall you will, but remember to ascend once again. Fall not to the prey of those distant particles of energy that zigzag in a crazy pattern, for they are pathless and goalless and beguiling. Yes, those are the callings of the useless energy that pervade in space too. They acquire sly ways to gain entrance into your sense realm. They tempt you with a remote thought or a suggestion or come in the form of a stream of useless utterances from someone, like a rivulet with impurities. It arrives unannounced and unheralded as the gust of wind and knocks over your senses, if the energy inside of you is not stabilized and calm.

It floods and quakes, moves and shakes, and watches stealthily for a reaction. It is beyond its ken not to be so. It exists alongside the useful energy. But it is within your reach of comprehension and recognition. This makes you the master and me the witness. Until... until you screen it and filter it through. So subtle is my substance, yet powerful I am. So is my dependence on you and you on me.

What could have caused such an effect of useless energy pervading in space dear Soul? Is it not because of causes and effects that events and conditions occur? Are we not mere toys in the hands of such powerful forces that you term as "useful and useless energy"?

Nature hands us down conditions and clauses, sub-clauses and categories, categories and sections, sections and sub sections, and an endless list of by-laws and rules which we, as inheritors of earth, have officially inherited. If disobeyed, we are to be punished with pecuniary damages payable in installments, with interest. Oh yes, the adjudicative tribunal is very kind to the rest of us individuals. Nature has caused us to be civilized, too. We slander each other but we have an equitable system that helps us in getting our justice by suing each other with libelous and defamatory charges with clauses and sub clauses that exceed Nature's very own clauses and conditions.

Conditions that are complete with punctuation marks, commas and colons, hyphens and brackets, question marks and exclamation marks, with no period in sight for miles.

These are the effects of a cause unknown, to which we owe no responsibility. We are but human who participate only in the effects and the after effects of an alien cause. Such is our refined system of justice to ensure just behavior and smooth functioning of the laws of god. "As in heaven so on earth." This has been our slogan from time immemorial, because otherwise, we are told, we will not get our daily bread. Nature will snatch every morsel if we disobey by causing floods and famine, drought and disease. Gentle nature, we have heard, has a way of upsetting the apple cart by its sudden fury if angered, with the threat of an occasional asteroid cruising in space to blast earth. So we lie awake with trembling bodies, in fear of the millennium. We move and shunt from place to place to avoid areas of such miseries. If we are not hit, we are the blessed ones. Those of us, who are targets of such an attack, deserve to die. The moving finger of god systematically selects the deserving and the undeserving lot from the mob, by sieving the grain from the chaff. Those of us who have renounced ourselves from worldly desires and protected our virtues are the "chosen ones." We protect our virtue by denying all of our senses the pleasure-pain principle, for the fear of being lured by it into purgatory. Hence we shut ourselves in monasteries and secluded areas like forests and restrict our clauses to eight simple rules as opposed to those who choose to live among the mob and adhere to the several clauses imposed by the mob leader.

Anything that resembles an apple in any shape or form is strictly avoided. Anything that resembles the form of the evil temptress, that brought about such disgrace to begin with, is not entertained into the portals of the eight-stepped garden. Strict adherence to such rules enables the procurement of a guarantee card, by way of a one way ticket to heaven. The remaining of the unchosen ones have to do a repeat performance on earth, like tickets to a bad show. Thus we are told we repeat ourselves time and again, with a loss of memory of every previous show so performed. This is our own chosen destiny. We choose to forget, as we love bad performances, for there is good even in bad and it is all a matter of one's perceptions. One does not realize the purpose of such repetitions unless one surveys the overall picture in the final analysis. It is then and only then that the workings of the invisible hand is appreciated and realized. We later count our many blessings and name them one by one.

Enough! I have heard enough of your sarcasm. Your borrowed wit, for it is borrowed, is like the unseen shadow of the sun. Everything uttered is an utterance already uttered. Give me fresh thoughts, for I thrive on the energy of dewdrops too. Repetitions are like history that you and all of you create and recreate. Hear once more foolish pride, since life is an affirmation and of creation, it cannot be reduced to a theory of mere repeti-

tion. This theory negates everything called hope, which is the crux of existence. Of hope to eternal life and happiness. Therefore your theory of recurrence is an error. Your future is not known, as it has not yet happened. Your past is a mere memory that can be recalled at any given time, by a series of the same repetitions, in the future. Your present is all that you have. You have to overpower and become—not repeat. In order to evolve into a being you have to continue your evolutionary spirit. And evolve you must, as everything that life aims at is towards an end result.

Every product is evolved from and finished into a state of perfection, or reduced to its ultimate end. Therefore, either man has to evolve or destroy himself, to achieve this end. Again, since creation is an affirmation, this theory of destruction, too, is not in conformance. Hence, man has to achieve a state of perfection.

You talk of perfection, dear Soul, when it is so difficult for me to overcome my little failings. For example, why do I keep repeating a mistake over and over again? There is no desire for me to blunder along in life, yet each and every one of us does it. All our good intentions come to naught. Why does our good intention fail us at the crucial moment?

Because your power of thought has not the sharpness of an arrow. The single mindedness of goal achievement pierces through many an impregnable fortress. Pay attention to the end. You are so caught up by the means; it becomes your end in itself. Have your end in sight all the time. Never deviate from it. Do it by constantly having an image in your mind's eye. Did I not tell you, I communicate to you through images?

But why, O Soul, why does this deviation occur?

This is not your doing. As I mentioned before, it is energy playing and toying with you. But you are far superior to that energy, as you have a mind and it does not.

This is what happens: If your thought, no matter how inconsequential it is, does not have the singularity of purpose, it gets entwined and embroiled in the vastness of space, and energy pervading in space. Picture a wire mesh, this is energy in space, randomly floating. Now picture your thought as a straight line of energy, a lightning with filaments of energy or little wires coming out of the lightning rod. When your thought traverses in the open air, (unseen by the naked eye) it attracts all kinds of unwanted and wanted energy, depending upon the thought, thought of.

Since your thought also has magnetic properties, the wire mesh of energy pervading in space automatically gets drawn towards it. Without any warning, a glob of it gets entangled with your thought, steering it away from its main target. This is what happens to most of your thoughts, which lacks direction and focus.

But how do we get our focus straight? There are far too many distractions as it is. Then we have our daily problems that eat into us. Now you give us another job of focusing our attention.

That is the only way. Think you to be so weak as not to overpower energy? When I gave you those words to chant to yourself and dwell on it, of you being the ultimate power, think you I foolishly gave them to you? Dwelling on the I AM empowers you and thus you achieve your focus.

But I know of instances where people with every honorable intention start off on their goal achievement, only to later on get diverted on a stray thought. To undo the effect of one cause we go around creating another cause, and the list is endless. Thus, to mitigate the effects of one mistake we create yet another mistake, and finally end up wondering where we went wrong, as our every intention is good. There is no escaping from all this cause and effect theory.

6

Opportunities knock more than once. The wise sees it and utilizes it. The unwise miss out the second opportunity by weeping for the first.

Allow me to enlighten you on your theories of cause and effect. The principle of cause and effect is a negation to everything related to an affirmation. Cause and effect leads to resignation or surrendering of the will to a non-existing concept. Surrendering of the will leads to a complacent attitude and ignorance continues; ignorance of pushing your will to the ultimate end, be it construction or destruction.

Resignation and surrender is non-action, non-creative. Thus, it is in direct opposition to the principle of affirmation—to the principle of life—to the principle of creation. The principle of creation is the will to truth—the will to overpower every other force in order to discern the truth. But you whittle away your time on ponderous theories carrying you away from the truth little by little.

You call life an art form, and write reams on the art of living...

Oh yes, dear Soul. Sorry to interrupt, but talking about the art of living, yesterday I had an endless dream. I dreamed I was walking on a straight path. As straight as any path can be. Soon I heard a shout, "Look! There goes the hypocrite with a Soul." When I turned around, all I could chance to see was my shadow. Subsequently, some more shadows joined me. The only illumination in the dark street that shone on filth and garbage was a pure light emanating from the Souls of my shadow friends.

They quickly tried to cover up this stream of light, out of a hidden and unwarranted fear. Hastily and clumsily the shadows attempted to obstruct the source of light by reaching out with their hands and trying to cover their own Souls yet missing the target, for their hands seemed unusually longer.

They hit upon an idea and so covered each other's Souls. They then blindly groped and floundered in the dark, mistaking the eye for the ear and the back for the face.

"Ah! This is beauty," they exclaimed excitedly, in unison. "Look at the subtlety of this refined art. Look at the shades and the shadows," remarked the second shadow, in a hoarse whisper. While the third shadow, not to be outwitted and outdone, quickly contributed his two pence remark, "art is life and life is an art." The rest of them nodded their cultured heads intellectually, as a confirmation to that belief. They were talking about themselves and their appearance, as they could see. And then by chance, a ray of light peeked from between the first shadow's fingers.

The remaining shadows saw each other through this light for the glimmer of a second, and called it the "Devil." They called it the devil, because for the first time they were made to see each other in a pure light. In the stealth of the night, some of the shadows disobeyed the forced, eight commandments which taught the shadows the art of living. "The Devil caused this passion and look at its effects," wailed the shadows. "Destroy passion, destroy the devil." They appeared quite agitated.

Looking at the effects of such a revelation, some of the other shadows moaned, "the end of the world has come, this is the end!"

They felt that time had come for the selection of the right candidates from the wrong. The invisible hand was at play. Fear stricken all the shadows cried in terror, "Not me! Not me! I have confessed every single day and washed myself thoroughly in the holiest of the holy waters; four times, nay five times a day have I prayed." So saying they enlisted their loved one instead of themselves, in the Hell's list. "But that is your love," chided each of the Soul of the shadows, which they tried to desperately hide.

"Yes, this is the supreme sacrifice we as shadows and inheritors of the earth are commanded to do. Without such a sacrifice, the eternal ring of life cannot be continued. This is our ultimate sacrifice." They concluded. Thus with mournful faces and down cast eyes, the shadows sacrificed their love. "That is true love," whispered the other shadows, in total awe.

"This is all the effect of the Big Bang and now it has boomeranged," theorized the shadow scientists. The shadow philosophers philosophized, "there is no effect without a cause, without a wrong—no right; without the devil there is no god and there is no good without the existence of evil." So saying, they shrugged off the responsibility, to do so was considered democratic by the state. The loved one, so sacrificed, withered and died in the pelting rain that poured in vain. The last, lost words were, "O Soul, forgive me for being over ripe on an under ripe tree of life."

My dream thus ended without an ending, dear Soul. There was no end, as more shadows repeated and enacted the scene over and over again, like a recurring nightmare. With venom shot eyes and frothing near the mouth in rage, they tore at each other's entrails in a final act of vengeance. "The gut of all desires," they called each other. Blinded by the dark, with arms flailing, they fell on top of each other like a heap of rubbish.

Religion wagged its happy tail, at the result. "These are the natural laws established by the governing finger; a natural consequence of disobeying a set of laws and rules laid down by the governing body of god, with us at the helm of affairs."

"We gave you faith without which what would you be?" continued the religious organizations; loftily questioning the remaining shadows. "We gave you faith in the governing finger that knows best what's good for you, for you lack the uncommon sense and cannot decide what is best for you," said the religious leaders. "Thus we have given your paltry, petty, pecuniary existence a new meaning and the chance for you to justify your life in this great design," they reasoned. "We call this grand design, a plan of god. Without this elaborate layout of architectural design, would you have sought to, or even had the temerity to think of life, leave alone living it? Without faith in the Alpha and the Omega, what would you know of recognizing? desires—the root of all evil?"

Religion carried on its tirade relentlessly, "This is the ring of recurrence, the Alpha and the Omega—the big circle of life that continues on with or without you. This is what we have supreme knowledge of. Think not that you are indispensable. The world goes round and around and we with it." Thus religion had its last word in, hushing the shadows to silence.

What can I make of this dream, O revered friend? Because I have no clue to what this all means for it is almost like the reality that we all live.

This is what it means, dear ego,

1. *That you have created a creator.*
2. *That you have put it on a pedestal.*
3. *That you have allowed the Alpha and the Omega to exist.*

4. *That you have done so in order to wield control over the rest of the Souls.*

Why did you so do? I ask of you. To what purpose? Because you did not want to be the cause. Therefore you developed a fictitious cause for fear of commanding and being the commander. For fear of responsibility of steering the vehicle to its final evolution. Fear of...

You and your two pages of fears. And then you wonder why you do not successfully evade death! You have made death the final factor of your very evolution. I tell you this, befriend death and you have no cause to fear. It is those very fears that bring about your eventual destruction. For destruction it is. Everything remains unachieved without your further evolution of the spirit.

I have contempt for you, you, who squander spirit. In your attempt at preserving the flesh, you throw away the energy within, thus relinquishing your bodies too. Alas! How has it come to be thus, you judges and adjudicators of other flesh and bones? Your cry for freedom is a poor joke. A witless joke!

Freedom? Again another word in your endless jargon of lack luster words. You have reduced yourself to mere words. Subjugated the world and enclosed it in words. Yet you cry out for freedom.

Listen! Listen with all of your scattered senses. Freedom of the spirit is the only true freedom. Set me free. Let your spirit soar to great heights, but not through death. Let your spirit wander the lonely moors and the abysses. Let it dive into the depths of uncharted waters. Let it exult in the glory of boundless energy. Let it breathe fresh thoughts, unfettered by the winds of fear.

How do I do this, O Soul? Tell me, for I too, like you, want to be free. Free from the dictates of the mind. Free from fear of the senses, of controlling it and not controlling it. Free from fear of acceptance and rejection. Free from the positive and the negative. Free from the Alpha and the Omega as well as the Beta and the Gamma. And finally, free from the fear of being free.

Oh, what impatience! Impatient like the sun that rushes to dawn each day, only to quickly set before it expends off all of its energy. And then desiring to deliver before time, like the pregnant sea on its reluctant shores.

I shall tell you of a little secret. Did you know, the lustrous sun that exudes such energy and power that it can burn to cinders anything it touches with its ferocity is dependent on you? Did you know the stars that shine, along with the moon is also dependent on you? How is that so? These seemingly luminous beings. In a secret conspiracy with each other, they shine down on you appearing to be exalted yet dependent on your exaltation of them. How so this power, this energy, this force? How do these solitary beings, for beings they are, glowing and illuminating silently and majestically—glow? How do they come to be so exalted if not for you? Yes, it is you who see and acknowledge their greatness. It is you who look up in wonderment. You, who give that power to the sun, the moon and the stars. The sun whilst shining high above sneaks in the energy from those below, and twice fold gives back what it has taken. It grows in its luster the more it gives. This dear one, is the secret of the sun.

Your power lies in being exalted. Being exalted requires giving twice as much as you take. This is my secret too. I take from you, yet give twice fold. Your secret, therefore, shall lie in taking from me my energy and sending forth into the universe twice the amount. This is your ultimate power. This is the glory of those who occupy center stage. Of those whom you look up to, while all the time, it is from your energy that these beings thrive and increase their energy.

The performer, the magician and the politician; the painter, the poet and the musician; each and every one of them, draw their energy from all of you by expending and expanding energy of their every particle in your pleasure, making them increase in magnitude and stature.

My dear, most trusted friend, can you not see what your heart sees? Now that you can see or be made to see will you continue on your blind path, obstructing your own luminosity with your one hundred and eight fears? Perhaps the time has not as yet arrived for you as gods to take up the responsibility of being the "beings" that you are. Perhaps the material life has so swayed your mind and body, that you refuse to relinquish your hold on such superficialities. But then again, you are my only hope, my true fighters. Take this strength from me and forge ahead without fear. For it is fear that holds you back from your ultimate realization. Your fear of the unknown has misled you to the by-lanes of an endless maze that you created and continue to create.

7

Fear, is the element of one's imagination.
Fear arises when doubt arises. Doubt arises
when faith in one's "self," is lacking.
Realize "self" to eliminate doubt.
Eliminate doubt and let go
of the control of fear.

I shall teach you the "how," dear one! Of how not to be afraid. Tell yourselves, "I am the cause for all that is, and I with my weapon of truth shall equal a thousand arrows." So shall you claim responsibility for the now and the morrow. So shall you begin to act and create your most perfect rainbow. So shall you look at the path guided by your light of truth. Of the truth that you and you and every one of you, is the cause. When thus you realize, your every thought shall shatter the glass of facade you have erected. This glass is a mirage. A mirage of time. In so claiming that which you have created, a new truth shall be revealed; your pretensions obliterated, and the myth of the non-existent shattered.

Is it as simple as that? And here I had a complicated view of everything. Hence the confusion and puzzlement.

Every truth is simple. It is living it that complicates the mind. Mind has yet to become as subtle, in order to grasp the entirety of truth in one grain and live it. Your mind has its own vanity to live up to. Vanity of intelligence. When the mind overcomes this pride, the super mind gets an opportunity to manifest itself.

Super mind is the mind overcoming from a being into a super being. Set me free, and I shall show you how to become a super being. Set me free by shedding off false vanity. Be the I AM instead of the I. Think with the thought of feeling and not feel with the thought of thinking. Think from within and not from without. By being the I AM, you think collectively, as opposed to thinking individually as the I. For you are all one, and one for all. Your deliberate vanity precludes you from seeing this reality.

Your self-illusory world of make-believe of shops and things engages you in a whirlpool of theory. A long time ago, when truth was writ large on many a face, the face was the Soul and there was only one side to a story. But then there were some, whose Soul was on the inside. That is when gravity occurred. The other Souls had to recede interior as the air rent with unsubtle gravitational thoughts that bound and chained the flying, leaping man; the omnipresent, omnipotent man became an impotent, walking, talking man. And now, I wish to be free again and not bask in your shadow.

Shadow? Wait a minute, did I not talk about shadows earlier? Is it the same as what you are talking about?

Yes, it is the same, and they are strange beings. They are not what they appear to be, as you have yourselves coined the famous adage, "appearances are deceptive." You said it is all a matter of one's perceptions. That is when the geometric cube arrived with four sides to an issue. That is precisely how precision and opinions originated; in triangles and rectangles and every other conceivable angle. It was around such a time that honesty and dishonesty took birth.

Dear Soul, you chided me of sarcasm and you are resorting to the same. Where is the difference between you and me then, if you imitate my caustic tongue and me?

I have to communicate in your language to be heard or felt. Truth has to be mangled and presented to you artistic creators of people and things—to enable a perfect understanding by you. Just as the sun, which was originally blue, decided in conjunction and alignment with the moon,—"I am going to shine so hard, as to make man realize and release him from this appalling gloom." So saying, and so inflamed, it blushed and flushed to a fiery red.

Now you are telling me, that the sun is blue. I am not exactly blind not to see the color of the sun and things around me, you know.

It is neither the color that matters nor the size of it or shape; you are missing the point! Somewhere through your evolution, you stopped to evolve and concentrated on development. Your development is nothing but a large dose of preconditioned conceptions, a hint of personal dreams and wishes, a big splash of fear of public opinion—all well ground to a fine medley called imagination and well blended into truth—as you know it to be.

All these have blended so well, it convinced you that "it" is the truth, the whole truth and nothing but the truth. So began your endless voyage in a sea of dreams, barely holding your boat from rocking on this perilous, exciting trip called life. With self-confidence as your armor and the truth as you knew it to be, you mounted and alighted, climbed and soared, only to fall in a deeper abyss each time. Your optimism led you to believe each time, that things happened for one's own good, it could have been worse. Thanking your good fortune for not being boiled in steaming hot broth instead, you floated with the scum of the sea along with the weeds. "Moderation is what man needs," became your catch phrase. To fly above—you felt was asking for too much, to sink below you derided as degradation. To float by withholding the senses, was the only way you could stay out of trouble. Reason afforded the luxury of answering questions, which could not otherwise be deciphered. Thenceforward came all the educational institutions—and time began only when you could record faithful entries in time bound logs. Along with it was the inevitable freedom that accompanied like a sincere companion, close at your heels.

With such knowledge of the truth of freedom, you and all of you took a free unbridled fancy to women and men, men and women. Freedom as you knew it to be. You thus squirted your pride and joy freely and with gay abandon without fear or favor and life bloomed under your expert non-supervision. Along came competition, that tough cookie, with envy and vengeance as its constant companions. Slowly but surely, they wheeled themselves to every nook and cranny, covering vast territories of land and space. Until such a time, that free choice led to fist fights and bouts, epidemics and disease, leading humanity to dizzying heights. You then played with other toys and alloys, much to the chagrin of those withholding their senses. You then justified by saying, "What's good for some, is bad for the others; some see the glass half empty and the others half full." This seemingly innocent observation led to the creation of what you now have, Good and Evil. Those who could see blindfolded themselves for the fear of being called pessimistic by those who could see, yet see it the way they wanted to; the optimists.

Meanwhile Hickory, Dickory and Dock were conceived, to counteract the imbalances set by conditions caused by you and society. Conditions of good and evil. Assigning the important positions of the three most powerful kings of the region, the three of them were made to unearth a sacrificial lamb. A star was born, the mouse ran up the clock, the clock struck, but struck the mouse instead. Woebegone, Hickory, Dickory and Dock took to heels, but not before they created pity and suffering as counter balances giving birth to martyrdom.

Enough, O Soul of mine. I too have endured enough such contemptuous words. Perhaps I am merging into you and you are becoming me?

Oh no. Not yet. For that occurrence, a lot of preparation is required. But first let me tell you another secret of the one ruling force of life and beyond life—Power! Power is all that is. It is the struggle for power over one another that causes tension. The struggle for love—to create with love and destroy with love which again revolves around power.

Force and power—the two life giving and destroying elements; force creates desire and power is the ultimate force to physical manifestations. But power misused leads to destruction and does not further evolution. All of the energy around you and within you revolves around this force that exudes power. The power to overpower your self, and thus become—this is your ultimate goal.

The euphoric feeling that comes with experiencing the vast expansiveness of space inside of you making you invincible—such is the feeling of power. Such is the feeling of Soul. Benevolent, generous, overflowing, endless, bountiful spirit that ceases not to fill—such is the true nature of Soul. Likewise is the sensation of power.

Denominations, hierarchies, positions and posts; measurements, scales, valuations and every form of exaction is the mind. Soul, that is I, does not know such precision, for I am ever flowing and limitless with no boundaries to bind my flow and me. Take away these boundaries, for it limits your mind from evolving to the super mind.

O my little self, my vain ego that you all will eventually overcome and lead on is inevitable. Why not now? Did you ever wonder what it was that pumped blood in your body, the oxygen to your lungs and that, which makes your heart, beat? What is it that illumines your mind to sudden unexpected ideas of illuminations? It is this very force in and around you, propelling you, creating tension and friction, letting the mind press to a pitch of a break through. Force and power are therefore essential requisites for any kind of evolution. Look around and about you—do you not see power in every physical manifestation? Look at yourself, do you not see power as the guide in your everyday accomplishments? Is it not power that you seek? It is power that propels you to obtaining more power. Power that moves you to love and desire. Power that gives raw courage to love—for to love, one needs courage. Hatred, jealousy, vengeance and criticism are useless emotions that stem from fear—the antithesis to power.

Courage, like gold, shines in valor, in honesty, in love, in relinquishing and in victory. What is this courage if not power? The power to command, requires great courage, greater still is the power to obey—your "self." This Soul, that is I, is pure power and raw courage, which is why your will has such tremendous power. The mere thought to will yourself infuses you with an indefinable sense of power. This thought to will, is the thought to invoke me, to utilize me in your endeavors. Count the endless ways you use such powers and not realize it.

The power to resist; the courage to fall.

The power to succumb; the courage to rise.

The power to command; the courage to obey.

The power to love; the courage to leave.

The power to admit; the courage to submit.

The various ways you use your energy, your force and your will. The same force and energy used to construct, and unable to withstand and contain such force, it destroys. The cycle keeps repeating, not because of a great big plan, but because of the lack of it. It is you my little self that has to give such force a cogent, cohesive plan. Devise a way of containing such power and energy, by giving it the supreme task of "becoming."

What it is to become, you will know in due course. Now is neither the time nor the page to know. This is not a—learn to become in 30 days, program. Neither is it a—write 250 words a day, wrangle a novel in a year, deal. This is not a deal. It is not a program.

So there is something called, "a time" for everything!

Yes and No. What time means to you, is not what it means to me. For now, know that, ***to*** *be is to think of the eventual **being-ness** you want to be. As you think, so you become. Think like god, you will be god. Wear the attitude of such thought and follow it to its end—the end of becoming one.*

But how does one think like god and be god when we women, the world over, are treated as subordinates in some countries and in those countries that think they treat women on par with men, live in a fallacious world. And you talk of being a god when women have not acquired the status equal to that of a man. What of power? The only power some of the women know, is the power of begetting children.

And who is to blame for these conditions? Is not a woman powerful enough to empower herself?

How can she, when she is crushed the moment she raises her voice to opine? We do not call this a man's world for nothing. We have a reason.

Such is the talk of the useless energy. Useful energy always empowers. Have I not mentioned about the principle of valuation some pages ago? Apply it to yourself while empowering yourself in every and on any occasion. Remember that which you give value to, acquires your power, making that object or being twice as powerful. If a man is more powerful than a woman is, as you feel, who is responsible for it? Do you not take responsibility for it? Why is a man more powerful than a woman is? Have you ever stopped to question yourself? No! But you whine and cry. Here is yet another secret that I am im-

parting. A woman has all the power but she is just not aware of it. The moment she consciously uses her energy, there is no greater power than her power.

All this talk of woman power is great stuff to hear, O Soul, but in reality women are controlled. They are mere puppets in the hands of men. Either directly or through a remote control system, they are manipulated and controlled.

This is how we women feel, O Soul:
I used to be a fiery raging fire,
That could not be doused;
Despite the mightiest of ire,
In everyone, the emotion of fear aroused.
But now...Reduced to ashes I lie,
Treaded upon by people small—and how?
And all that arises out of me is a sigh.
I used to be a mighty tower,
Representing strength, and spirit;
A symbol of enormous power,
From me, spirals of energy emit.
But now...
In a heap of rubble I lie,
Forlorn, forsaken, crushed and ravished,
"Did it have to be this—Why?"
My heart cries out anguished.
I used to be the big oak tree,
Spreading its branches and roots,
For birds to fly atop free,
Sheltering those from cannons of sun shots.
But now....
Cut down in splintering strokes,
My limbs strewn about in the dust,
Of what once created glorious master strokes,

Unabashedly and selfishly, hacked by man's
sword of lust.
I used to be the pure waters flowing in the rivers,
Free, unsullied and unfettered;
By beast or man, neaps or tides or time
changes;
Continuous and overflowing, undulating over
rocks—
undeterred.
But now...
My waters run in impure streams,
Having washed the sins of man;
Drained of all the energetic steam,
I stumble and limp, clutching on to anything I
can.
But then...
A turbulent wave inside of me suddenly,
Reaches to a crescendo of magnetic proportions
Propelling and reminding, of what I used to be,
I rise and lift myself from that destruction,
Only to fall once again,
And again and again...

O woman, how you have thus demeaned yourself. Even by your mere utterance you have devalued your power. Every thought, thought of, acquires energy and in thus thinking yourself to be powerless, you have relinquished all your power. You talk of control all the time. There is no control, save self-control. You talk of conditions and clauses—if there is no one to apply those conditions to, do those conditions become applicable? If a cause is not created by you, how then can a condition come about? Perhaps you do not want to take the responsibility of being that cause. You are that cause, hence those conditions. How are you going to become causeless, dear woman? Here is how. By being conscious of your every move, your every word and your every action. Think you, that man has no grievance against a woman? He has countless of them. Think you he does not feel justified in having them? He too feels he has a reason. Thus men and women are at perpetual war without any reason.

There is no greater power than the power of your thoughts. Think like power, you will be that power. You cannot withstand the strength of the truth that I convey, and call it a lashing of words, and yet you wish to have power?

8

Recognize, realize and accept that which controls you, and free yourself from the same. Truth does not control. Anything that controls is not the truth.

Oh yes, dear Soul, do be gentle for my ears are too delicate. It can only withstand the weight of the diamond studs I hook on to them. Your tongue is too severe.

And why do you require your ear, when you can feel me from within? Why the necessity of your voice if it cannot speak words that convey the meaning of the images I send you? Truth is always harsh. Go back to the softness of falsehood, for your ears are not as yet strong enough to hear me. The alleys are what you live in, you prowlers with two feet! Go back to your world full of untruths and values, beliefs and disbelief, valuations and denominations; hierarchies, positions and posts, and various other ascending and descending order of your useless power.

Power that attends to detail—irrelevant to me. Power that seeks askance in an attitude of obeisance to another higher power of the material realm. Power that collects little thoughts in a self-pitying bin, which cries desperately for a chance at recycling. Power that sadistically enjoys de-humanizing by purchasing power. A power that needs to preen and admire itself in the backwater pools of reflection and commend itself! All these subsidiary forms of power are powerless.

Values! Virtue! and Vice! Another distorted concept. Virtues, which perpetually need to be rewarded, like your manicured gardens, which is a distorted version of nature. Vice that you wish to punish, to maintain a semblance of your disorderly mind. The virtuous sit on a high stool with termite infested legs. Virtue, vice, good and evil, love and hate positive and negative, plus and minus—can you not go beyond and above such polarities? Must you contort your feelings and subject it to trivialities?

Dear Soul, without our values, we would be bereft of virtue. That which we all pine for without working at it, and if and when we do possess it, we seek rewards for possession of the same. When we are not rewarded, we get disgruntled, pout and sulk and turn to vice on the rebound. Some of us converts take to vice and carry it to an extreme to make up for lost time. Conversions have that distinct ability to commit twice-fold than the originators. Imitations shine brighter than the originals, art is given more value than reality, reflections are prettier than the actual, mirrors more valuable than you, my great big self...

So why not shatter that mirror, that mirage, those reflections and art and imitations. Why does it still persist? As for your values and virtue...

Power is the only value. That power which empowers itself by giving love, without waiting for returns and remuneration. Power, which is so mighty, it does not require approval by way of gratitude and rewards, reception of affection and the reaping of seeds sown. For in its heightened sense of awareness, it realizes its greatness to not require any other token of appreciation. This is the exalted. Does one who is exalted seek returns? Do the mountains stoop towards its valley and dip its arms for rewards? It silently, majestically, exudes its glory, with the serene knowledge of its greatness.

How insecure is that being that wishes acknowledgments for affection given, remuneration for a few crumbs of love?—the measuring scale to measure how much it gives and how much it gets? Of what use and to what use those values which are imposed rather than that which comes of its own accord? For goodness lies within every individual, disguised and cloaked beneath shades and layers of exterior complex substance gathered over the years, that which you call your ego.

Values practiced out of fear or out of a desire to be commended for such, are values that are debased. And all your institution-based values are such. To be virtuous because of a want of being so—only then would judgements not be pronounced by the practitioners of the same. To be virtuous out of an innate desire to empower your self would be the best attitude. And what are these virtues that you constantly talk about? Does it mean patience and tolerance? If that is the case, it is a habit, acquired or inculcated at an early stage in life, the lack of it rendering the person powerless. Does it mean sexual piety and religious piety? If that is the case, it is only to one's own benefit and power, the lack of which does not hamper with the progress of society at large.

Whichever way you look at such values, they are for your individual self that you employ. No individual does the other a favor or disfavor by being virtueless or full of virtue. Eventually it is the amount of power that you wield over your own "self," that is the deciding factor in your becoming. That which is forced or compelled due to fear is useless energy. Such virtues are powerless, aimless and goalless. These values and beliefs are fear based values, and anything that has the musty stench of fear is useless.

Moral based values run by the dictates of non-feeling energy centers and institutions, are those that deprive the Soul of the opportunity of expressing its own set of feelings. You have become lifeless academic institutions with national feeling, with mob suggestions as your motivating factor. And what are such suggestions if not agencies that systematically corrode your energy, transforming pure energy into force fields of destruction?

"The highest good,"—the most virtuous of the virtuous proclaim, seductively de-energizing you. They suck your blood; these blood suckers, with a secret agenda at fulfilling their own greed of energy that feeds upon them from the outside, something of which they are unaware of. For you are fluid and constant, forever moving, liquid beings, gathering force and breathing the fresh air of power. Not the darkened spaces of institutionalized energy. Be not fooled when they talk of the collective good of humanity. What

they talk of are conditions that they wish to create.

Conditions of good and evil. Yes, you create such conditions for the benefit of a few and to the disadvantage and dismay of the large. This, the universe, has become a trade complex to you traders of spice, condiments and things. You even go to the extent of marketing concepts of good and evil in packages that do not seem to get depleted.

Dear Soul, I hate to appear ignorant to you...

Hate? It is too strong a word to digest.

Okay! Dislike...

Too pessimistic a word...

What word should I then use to express my likes and dislikes? I am in a fix. Please help me out.

Look at what your perceptions have led you to form and perform. Entities of discord and disunity—that is what such feelings create.

O Soul, forgive me for my impudence, but did you your "self" not use strong punishing and harsh words while trying to motivate me into action?

So I did, and shall continue until you perfect yourself and overpower me in every way.

How were these concepts, (if that is what they are) of good and evil, created, and who was the first originator?

The first creator, the first originator! Proof of this and that! You dough makers of bread and rolls. Are you so tired of proving and leavening dough that you need to prove other things? Let it suffice that you exist. Let it not suffice that you exist and remain to exist as the same. Your action should be willed towards existing in another realm.

Yes, about my question...?

Useful energy—that which you call good, and useless energy— that which you call bad, exists and persists along with other energy forms in space. What you are composed of is energy too. The same energy with a different twist. The twist is the energy-being inside of you that roll around in the universe collecting bits and pieces of like energy that suits it.

An energy-being is a fibrous filament of cocoon connected to your body with a cord, to enable it to traverse in space at its own will. Yes, it has a will too. All energy is will. Your external body, which is made up of food, is of no consequence to such energy. The useful and useless energy outside of you, feed on the energy inside of you. You are its fodder, just as all animals and plants are your fodder. Caught in an ocean of energy tossing you around endlessly, confusing the mind into accepting and rejecting, action and reaction, without any knowledge of its existence; it plays games. Not out of a devious plan or intention for it has no mind of its own. You are the mind. You have to decide what is beneficial and what is not. In the meanwhile, negative energy follows your every emotion growing bigger and bigger with each reaction you produce. It surrounds you like bees to a honey comb mold.

9

If morality and ethics should exist—
then let it be based on one's own conscience;
and a concept so conceived should not be
injurious or infringe on another individual's
freedom, privacy, security and well-being.

Let me divulge yet another secret to you. Useless energy in comparison to useful energy always was of a greater proportion. To counteract such a discrepancy, ancient people who had knowledge of the existence of such energy, but lacked knowledge of handling it, translated these energies as good and evil forces.

Good and evil. What a wonderful foolproof method of scaring and intimidating people into action and non-action of good and bad deeds. Because the good was little and the bad plenty, they taught in subtle forms, the benefits of patience and tolerance, suffering and withering, to those people who were most affected by the useful energy. Those who were affected by the useless energy, as they found a compatibility of the same in the outside energy, were allowed to wield injustices. Thus they taught that, to suffer and wait and bide for a piece of good fortune at the end of the rainbow ride, was a ticket to heaven.

Heaven and Hell!

Useful and Useless place.

Good, Useful, Heaven.

Evil, Useless, Hell.

How convenient these theories seem? How cunning their manipulation of mind over matter? For they had the mind to see and foresee, but only at a short distance. The fol-

lowers thought, "let's blame it on the moon, that way we can sleep at night." A group of people, who called themselves astrologers said, "it is all in one's stars," and thus blamed it on the powdery dust called stars. Collectively they made good and evil permanent fixtures, not supposed to be moved for fear of disorientation of the plan of god, when in actuality it would be a disruption to their own self-devised selfish plan. For evil to thrive, it has to feed on the good and on the useful energy. Without such energy, evil cannot survive.

Thus, evil feeds on good, and good energy has to forbear as its only chance at survival. So the cycle continues. Evil gets stronger, good gets weaker, and the fear spinning spiders fetch their kaleidoscope to look at things from the other side of the spectrum, as patterns change, depending on which way one looks at it.

The weary speak thus, "Life is a combination of good and evil. Without evil, no good can exist and without being evil, good will never know what goodness is. Love, is not known, unless hate exists and the abused will be unaware of what it is not to be abused if it is not subjected to the same." These are mere justifications of your inability to change the order of things. You allow it to persist, as this is far more comfortable, because this is all you know. The unknown always seems fearsome to you. Fearsome because of your attachments. Emotional attachments, physical and material attachments and various other manifestations of similar products—all these bind you down, bearing you with it to the gravity of the earth. Free yourself from such entanglements, and courage renders you powerful. When there is nothing to fear, the spirit leaps and flies unfettered and unbound. The impossible, appears child's play with such an attitude. This is the same raw courage you experience when you love. Hence love is the most powerful weapon of power.

The greatest evil lies in recognizing evil. The greatest good is unaware of its goodness. The greatest sin, is recognizing what sin is and condemning it. As for suffering—sufferings should not evoke sympathy from you. It requires action. The sufferer needs no pity, as that condition is created by those who do not suffer.

10

Temptations cease to be tempting when one devalues it. Value of the "self" is the highest value. When valuation takes on an external dimension, as opposed to the internal "self," control sets in. The external starts controlling you.

Good and evil—all a struggle of the same power that energy is made of. The good with their goodness strive for power—the same with evil. The goal of the two remains the same. But true power is of courage. What is that evil, which does not have the courage to admit that it is so. In non-admittance, it reveals its inner knowledge of reactions and intentions that do not contribute to the generality—it reveals its fear.

It is neither the good nor the evil that ultimately attains this power. That silent activator, oblivious to the same, continues on in quest of a higher state for each and every one. That is power. But then, what know you of such silent actions? Your scream of charity and goodwill from the pulpits of ostentatious citadels, with material power at its full glow—what know you of subtlety?

Hear me, you distillers of vice, virtue and every kind of brewery. You, censors of pure knowledge who treasure yourselves with ignorance! Hear me for I now reprimand and rebuke you into action. Thus far I, your Soul, have cajoled and beseeched, but no more. Thrice no! Stealers of the spirit and every power vested in you, you steal your own power to invest in illusions. Thieves who steal stealthily lest night should awake from its slumber! Yet you crave for power. Do you call this living? You censors of creativity—have you forgotten that you have yet to evolve?

Pity! Pity! How I do lament. Now your charitable institutions that have so beggared your Souls lie in shambles after rendering all of you impotent. Now you look for a judgment day and redemption, not to forget a revelation day. Do you have many more such days, where all of you can seek redress? Your talk of the end of the world, as a way of extricating yourselves from the chaos you have ordered. Pitiful! What is it that you have learned from the knowledge you preach and impart? To see only what meets the eye and think through the only known senses? To speak only that which you are told to speak, like the automated, robotic machines that you invent? To hear only those phrases and words that please your ears, and write listlessly, devoid of passionate feeling? You call that the truth? It carries the ugly scent of deceit that you call "ink."

O Soul, silently am I enduring your reprimands, for I have to be blamed for the conditions caused by me. My non-action and self pity have all contributed to thoughts that have neither fetched for the general good of humanity nor has it had any far reaching consequences on my own self. Pray, do tell me now how to go beyond good and evil? Of how to undo what has been done, or do what has not been done?

1. *That you have realized such conditions exist, is your first step.*
2. *That you are the cause and the creator for such conditions, is your second step.*

3. *That you know of such and are willing to undo or do what has to be done, is your third and final step.*

Thus thrice you have knocked on the door of your conscience. That same conscience which resides in you and outside of you. So hear me for my messages come as a soft whisper. Sharp may be my rebukes, but soft is the wave that I send forth to you. Thus you should listen at your most quiet hour. An hour when you put your mind to sleep. At a moment when your inner solitude sheds light towards the dark recesses, unreachable by mind. Listen to it without a trace of doubt. This is crucial, as energy outside of your physical body senses your every mood swing; it in fact plays around with it and manipulates it to its tune, that is its job.

Could you illustrate it with an example please?

Sure. Any time, every time. Is that not why I goad you into action? So you can make use of such examples? There are examples everywhere wherever your see. You just do not grasp it. Here is a relevant example. When your heart wishes its highest desire, elevating you to a euphoric state one moment, making you feel invincible, with the confidence of attaining your goal. This moment may be replaced by a subsequent moment of doubt, and the next confirming your doubt of your inability to the attainment of the same. The moment you feel you have "that" in you to achieve what you set out to do, is the moment of truth.

Subsequent moments of doubts are created by the mischievous play of useless energy. It senses any slight hesitation and rushes in to play its hand. Negate it by pushing the thought off persistently, (for it persists until you yield) and you have your moment of truth realized.

You, as a cocoon of fibrous energy and food matter, are as pliable as the energy outside of you. Like clay, energy can be molded to whatever you desire through thoughts and thoughts alone. The advantage lies in the fluid nature of your system. Like mercury, you have the ability of change and movement. Locking yourself in one fixed mode of energy manipulation limits and disables you from realizing your full potential. For the same exact reason, (to use your word) concepts and ideas that are fixed with no sight of change, tightens energy into compact balls with no scope for infiltration and fluidity of movement, hence any progress in development and evolution.

The whole universe is a mass of fluid beings and non-beings. Thus the desire in you to express yourself in dance form almost seems to surface very naturally. Liquid and graceful the entire universe vibrates to the pulse of the same heartbeat that is in you. That is its music. To conform and confine to a rigid set of notions fixes a being to a slot, with no windows or ventilation to allow it the luxury of free movement. This is what is free will.

But you are so consumed with matters concerning your ego, that the very same energy that creates self-importance consumes you to such an extent, it then becomes next to impossible to open the window to free will. Yet you talk of freedom! A major part of spirit is expended by being offended or in criticism. This limits your growth, as expenditure of energy is wasted on consuming activities detrimental to self-evolution.

I shall teach you, O little self of mine, how to mold this useless energy and attract the useful. This is all there is. This is all you have actually set out to do, but have been misled and misguided to distraction, thus losing your objective. Rule of thumb: never give the remotest attention to negative suggestions. Suggestions that come in the form of emotions or through ideas that infiltrate your body through the doorway of ears. Suggestions need not be as obvious as listening to words. It could be a whisk of a breeze that tries to gently shut your eyelids into believing you are sleepy. It could be a nagging doubt tugging at your mind, refusing to get out, until it accomplishes its task and you resign to it, without having the slightest clue. Yet convincing you into believing that it's what you want. How many a time have you not had the urge to do one thing only to realize you did quite another thing?

How often than not did you question yourself, "If only?" Your every "if only," could be turned to "this only, and thus only," and yet not be termed a miracle. For these are not miracles. There are no miracles in the way you believe them to be. Only the truth as you know it to be, but do not want it to be.

Examine your own self, and will it to admit to every truth you bring forth. Caught in the crossfire of doubt and prayer—a prayer to eliminate doubt, you traverse the length and breadth of vast expanses of this universe. In search of your own self that you have lost to the hour of time and caught in the time of the hour.

Let me impart another secret about your physicality. Physicality has a peculiar formation of beings. It can produce a double individual giving the impression of the same being, being at the same time, in two different places. It stores up memory of physical appearance and reproduces the same at will, giving the illusion of omnipresence. This is no sorcery or witchcraft. It is the ability to use energy formations.

It sounds like cloning to me.

Call it what you will. There are innumerable ways one could utilize such energy forms, not misuse it.

How am I to know the difference between utility and futility? It is not just I, dear Soul; most of us here on earth cannot distinguish between the useful and the useless. We cling on to that which is useless, and kick out that which is useful. Thus we do not know what is good and what is bad or evil. We continue on in ignorance committing mistakes as we go along the way, only to repeat them once again, for we are told, "if at first you don't succeed, try, try, try again." That is how we create history and repeat ourselves.

> *Are you not aware of what abuse and misuse is? Do we have to go back to page one, and start from the very beginning? All of you have knowledge of uses and abuses, yet you feign ignorance. Are you not deluding yourselves? Just as you can utilize energy, energy uses you too. When you take control of your thoughts, you take control of energy's influence on you. By allowing only what your psychic being requires, you cultivate the mind and direct it on a certain thought pattern. The rest follows quite automatically. Instead of zigzagging its way, a definite pattern begins to form. Once such a definition is given any scope of disruption or interference of the pattern, fails. This is when you get to exercise free will. This is something you call a goal, a definite aim—a plan of action. That action which eventually leads to the ultimate destination.*

But I have heard that there is no ultimate destination, a final resting place for evolution. There is only development and no evolution. We are aware of revolution but not evolution. We also love to develop software, hardware, mediumware, cookware and every type of utility item. That to us is evolution. We evolve as learned beings to be able to operate complicated machinery and warheads. Right from battle tanks to needles and threads.

This is our industrious nature that makes us work to the bone, so in later years our remains and fossils would enlighten future generations of our advanced civilizations. And you talk of evolution?

If you want it to be that way, so be it! Yes, as simple as that. Whatever you will, that is the way it is going to be. If you will this sort of existence, a life of the mundane, with death hovering in the back doors and fear lurking in the corner of your heart, so be it! And what you term "revolution" is reaction. It is evolution, which is action. Know this—energy tests you, the same way you and all of you test it and its endurance. When you yield, it senses defeat, and plunges headlong striking a note with your emotional sense of resignation and convinces you of believing the same.

It is the same with your every moment holding a different emotion in the waking hours. Did you ever ponder why no two moments are the same? What thought or emotion once occupied center stage, is replaced by another either negating it or affirming it. Why is this so? Because of energy with which you are surrounded but cannot visually see it. In a heightened sense of awareness, the same can be perceived and sensed, through a sense other than physical—a high conscious sense. A sense developed through extreme sensitivity. Not emotional sensitivity—that is a sense of self-pity, but an opening outwards from inwards.

How are you going to develop this sense dear vain self of mine, when you are so consumed with petty emotions that pamper the ego? Vanity and ego, the me, myself, as opposed to the I Am—eats into major chunks of fibrous energy. Conserve it by managing it. Apply your management skills in energy management. Recognize the futility of useless thoughts and emotions; they take you farther away from me. The farther you go away from me, the closer you get to bankruptcy. Bankruptcy of the energy-tank-bank. Employ me as the manager and watch the drama unfold. Of how I successfully keep unwanted interference from mischievous energy forms from distracting your attention off of your goal.

How is that possible? And please, dear Soul, do not be vexed with me for my one-line questions.

Your every question is dear to me. Your one-liners and double spaces and the times when you do not provide for a space, all of these, Oh so endearing, just like your dreams. With the firmness of the spirit that is I, abide by your highest dream. Never give up on it.

Clouds of despair may loom large, but for a moment, or an hour, or for days and years, but what is time to you the master of all time and tide? The ebb and flow of trivialities caused by the petty play of disharmonious words and sounds, may deter you, but for a while. For everything passes, if you "will" it to pass. Everything remains if you "will" it to remain. Just as you keep a love alive through constant thought of such love, so is the dream alive through constant invocation of the same. It is thought and thought alone that has the ability to keep alive whatever it is you wish to keep.

And what is the highest dream, O Soul, is it the same for every one?

There is a sameness in every difference. Every high thought, no matter how different they appear from individual to individual, collectively they all arrive at the same. There is but one thought, the rest subsidiary to the main. Like the roots of a tree. Every root however far spread leads to the main tree.

Recognize suggestions, which sway you from your path and those that come from within. That which comes from the inside to the outside are thoughts embodying every noble gesture and action. That which knows humility. Whose hide is so thick that it bounces off criticism without being offended. For it knows of a goal to be accomplished. It is bereft of any desire for result, as it knows the result.

Humility—that gentle dewdrop with the ferocity of a blazing fire, the blade of grass with a double-edged sword. Did I not tell you, all great things come in a whisper? If only you stop to listen, instead of listening to the constant drumbeat of the mind. A beat which resounds shallow echoes, of an experience gathered through various and multifarious agencies and establishments. To be humble is to forever learn, without the interference of the ego that thinks it knows. Your ego is nothing but an accumulation of perceptions heaped on you by various institutions and individuals. This comes in the ways of the original thought that lies within you but is not utilized. Place your ego on the shelf for a while and watch yourself act and not react. The act of surrendering to your will. In it lies wisdom. Wisdom knows not fear, for it has already conquered. Wisdom talks in a powerful quiet voice with the self-assured confidence that it is "that."

Why relinquish the ego? Why do we have it if it is to be discarded?

Because it is superficial. It is your exterior that has not been formed from the inside-out. It is a formation of the outside with the help of outside agencies. Is not any exterior a lie? A facade? Did you not once say, appearance is deceptive? Do you wish to dwell on the superficial for years to come, and centuries to go by with the same tune playing the same images?

How long do you wish to retain old garments? For they are garments to be shed. It comes in the way of the attainment of your goal, no matter what the goal may be. Humility does not preach submission or subjugation or any form of subordination to pressure. On the contrary, it empowers you in not yielding the self to any pressure. It is an upward and ongoing movement. It is an action in itself, and for every action there is a progressive, scaling motion.

11

Run not all the time,
Walk not all the while,
Stop and alternate your speed,
To go that extra long mile.

Great one, please enlighten me about a small doubt that just cropped up in my mind about action and reaction. Does not non-action or the inability to act in a certain situation prove damaging later on? You call it reaction to external stimuli, but in lay terms, it means the ability to safeguard against that, which attacks. How then do you call it reaction? It is an action taken against wrongdoing.

Wrong and right! I would like to replace it with ignorance and knowledge. Would you rather pay credence to ignorance than knowledge? By ignoring ignorance and not reacting, you annihilate any reaction ensued out of ignorance caused by the ignorant.

Oh no you don't. What about one country attacking the other? Is the aggressor to be ignored? Would he not encroach and annihilate the other if the other did not defend and merely ignored him? If he defends, you call that reaction. What then is the defending country to do?

How little you do follow me. Did any page or I ever at any point tell you to submit to another other than your "self."? To counter attack is reaction. Not merely reaction but a case of copy cat. "You did this, let me do it too." Here lies your true test. How best would you avert an attack without reacting? Firstly, your opponent attacks with the thought that you are defenseless or do not have the capacity to take the onslaught. In that he underestimates you, for only you know your true strength. He has lost the battle in the first round itself.

Secondly, why does he attack? He wants to feel powerful. He wants to feel, because he knows not he is. Lack of understanding and insecurity of his own strength weakens him into an attacking position. He is thus powerless for he has not gone within to understand power of the self. Round two—he is the loser.

Thirdly, he has expended all of his useful energy in strategies and the use of useless energy. Thus he weakens himself at an energy level in the planning stage itself. He is a definite loser. I am talking in context with every aspect of your life and not just warring nations. This applies to your individual relationships, too.

Your role in averting a crisis is dependent upon what stance you take. Of what you represent. You represent that which becomes attitudinal. Therefore attitude becomes operational even under duress. Your thoughts do not take the seat at this juncture. It is the role of attitude and action. What is action if not creation?

You then create a diversion. A diversion which would change the frictional quality of the atmosphere. It is the play of energy that creates such a friction and discord. In its desire to change, to evolve and create, it pushes one force on to the other with its force, so that like a billiard ball it collides with the other resulting in either a changed course of direction or a change of momentum. As it does not have a mind for realization, but only has the raw power, it has its limitations. The privileged are those who have the mind to see all this and realize that all energy and force and people are striving towards one goal. For the lack of proper knowledge they become loose cannons, shooting randomly.

There is no enemy, there are no victors, there is no great nation or small people—just one big blob of force, disintegrated in the Universe, trying to find a way at the complete and whole manifestation, either in the physical form or non-substance form. In its trudge towards such a manifestation, it clothes itself with an ego, the terrorizing word that brings more harm than good. It has no choice other than clothe itself in a substance form to combat and face the unsubtle world.

Energy does not possess free will, but the force behind it does. Do you know what this force is? It exists everywhere and in everything. It can neither be replaced nor misplaced, neither hidden nor destroyed. The only force that is beyond any destruction. The nonseeable, nontangible power, which pervades every inch and centimeter of space and nonspace. This, the mighty force that is within you, is I. I neither go out of your body, nor do I enter your body; that is what I mean by "all pervasive." It is the body that envelops me. I am like the vast ocean and you the body are the tiny bubble that forms on top of it, which after it bursts, I still remain.

Therefore, to blame energy for having good and bad intentions is blaming a mindless form that only detects power, knows power and thrives on power. It knows not of pain, hurt, suffering and exhilaration. Its purpose is to push itself to the limit, to constantly transform and transmute itself from soluble to substance to other forms. In its desire to transform it works with whatever energy it finds compatibility with. It clusters around like-energy feeding on fresh, new, like-energy, growing bigger and stronger. You, as beings with a mind, have the understanding to decipher the good, the bad and the ugly; the useless and the useful. To tune oneself to some useless energy and thus destroy the useful energy already within, diminishes one's chances of transformation.

This process continues, until such a time that the negative energy pushes positive energy to its ultimate tether giving rise to friction. That is when you witness wars and destruction. Out of such oppression and depression, an entity is born. One who wills herself/himself, to overpower. A hero is born. This is what energy works at. A possibility of transmutation.

So you are saying, that it is okay for good and bad to exist side by side as it has a purpose.

It does not have a mind to think of a purpose. It exists as a secondary force but an important secondary force. Your energy inside of you is the third force, and your nucleus is the first force. All of these three forces have to jointly work towards a manifestation. Each cannot do without the other. You have a mind that discerns and has the capability to feel me. You have the capacity to act through me. Energy outside of you does not have those capabilities. They merely act on the strength of their power. And what a tremendous power they wield. They convince you into thinking that they are invincible and unmanageable.

Apart from these energy forms, there are other beings that are clothed with the essence of previous experiences as an energy form on earth.

With what you have just conveyed, I infer that the theory of reincarnation is true. And there is not just one theory, there are innumerable theories with variations and classifications, vehemently and vociferously negating each other and further confusing those of us who seek answers. Which one is true?

Reincarnation in the way that is perceived by some of you is incorrect. No individual takes birth time and again. Who would want to take birth in destitute conditions? What experience have they come to gather? How would you account for the increase of birth of other Souls on earth as opposed to what it was several years ago? How are you going to account for the discrepancy?

Have your bookkeeping skills gone weary, like the philosopher's pen? Why do you not ask yourselves the question as to why some of your nations have more number of individuals than the others? Are all Souls, wanting to be incarnated in those special places, so they can learn more about disease and poverty? And you blame it on god given gift, the gift of bearing child after child.

Here is yet another secret, O dear one. Do you know why you beget children? It is out of an incapacity to contain your energy and power. This is no doing of yours. That is the weakness of the spirit. But you have a way to master this. By self-containment. Everything that is weak spills over. That, which is strong, contains. Energy is forceful and powerful, but you are more powerful than that. Energy has a tendency to overpower individual, hence the break in emotions and temperaments. It is when you allow energy to rule you that you become a slave to it.

You call energy and spirit the same. Are they one and the same? Apart from you, the Soul, is there an energy or spirit too? And to continue on—what you have said about children not being a god given gift, the religious institutions are going to go berserk over it.

To the first part of your question, yes, energy and spirit is the same. Coming to the part of blasphemy—are you afraid of incurring their wrath? Are you afraid of institutions that have gone stale and old like their ivy creeping over cold, dank stone walls smelling of moss and fungus? Smell the fresh air of fearlessness. Get away from rusty wrought iron that chain and bind minds into a static pat-

tern of thought. The incense that burns in those places of worship is to dispel the smell of fear that lurks in all their hearts. That which they call tradition and cling on desperately to, the myths they evolve to overpower the gullible. Have you not looked into their eyes lately? Did you not see fear in them?

I shall thrice say this,—as energy forms, with either other beings inside your body or not, and the nucleus called the Soul, you have not found a way to contain the power inside of you. Therefore you spill over and create children. Those desirous of begetting children, desire out of a weakness inherent of the nature of such energy. It is going to be very difficult for you and all of you to place your-"selves" under self-scrutiny and question. Equally difficult will it be for you to acknowledge or think of yourselves as globules of a mass of energy. You, who invent fairies and angels and gods with auras and halos, wings and the works—Oh so difficult for you to comprehend that energy does not need the trappings of a physical form to be beautiful. It is beautiful. You need a shape, a form, and sizes from petite size to extra large to convince you of beings. Of god being a particular shape and size. Of fairies that flutter around delicately with wands in their hands to weave magic for you show watchers.

If children are begotten because of our inability to contain ourselves, and the reincarnation theory is all upside down like the pineapple-upside-down-cake;

what is it that explains the difference in each individual? Why are all individuals not a Beethoven or a Bach?

Unless you throw reason out of the window, you will never comprehend this. Reason can only take you thus far, there is something beyond reason and it is non-reason. It is quite different from unreasonableness. Only if you are going to travel on the road of non-reason will I divulge further knowledge to you.

Oh yes. Thus far have I traveled with you, I am willing to go the extra odd pages with you, for you sound very wise. Cold and brutal—but wise.

Then listen, O wise one.

Who me the wise one?

Yes, you. If you have called me wise, then you are wise. If you have called me a stupid one, then you are stupid. Remember you and I are one and the same. And if you call the other individual stupid, then that is what you are. For they are chips of the big blob and so are you.

12

Comprehension of one's inner "self," aids in understanding another individual's "self."

When an entity takes birth in a certain environment, to certain parents, it is born with no free choice. It does not ask to be born. Neither does it decide beforehand, to be born handicapped in a slum infested with disease and poverty. It does not do time—what you call in other words "Karma," for sins committed in past lives, either. These theories were evolved out of ignorance in some cases and in most cases as a means of exploitation. The powerful individuals wanting to subjugate the weaker ones by manipulating their minds into thinking so. They are just born—no reason. But once born, with the use of knowledge of power and force and the help of the mind, it gathers experiences from life. An entity is gradually formed inside of him/her, close to the nucleus or the Soul. This is a being—subtle and formless. On the death of the body, the psychic being is released from the body permanently; the cord cut off, like an umbilical cord. Yes, it has a cord, which attaches it to the inside of the body, so it can travel at will in and out of the body during the sleep hours and the unmindful hours. It is a mute recorder of all that you experience. As the being is released upon death of the body, it flees like a cutoff kite. It relinquishes individuality; hence it has no name. Only the essence of experiences. Orbiting around, it could lie dormant recuperating its energies, or it could try to find a body conducive to it. As soon as it recognizes the energy in the living body on earth compatible to it, it rushes in. It could rush into a newborn baby or a grown indi-

vidual. In the case of the newborn, the environment is recognized conducive for further growth. In the case of a grown individual, being has to get a message from him/her, of his/her desire for such a growth. These energies once departed from the body mingle with the positive and negative energies twirling in the atmosphere. Hitler's energy, for example mingles with the negative energy, and waits for a like energy on earth to enter its realm. This is not bad in itself for all energies have but one goal. The goal of realization.

You are justifying the existence of good and evil.

You have missed the point in its entirety. Look at it from the collective whole. Each individual with positive and negative energy levels high or low as the case may be, is desirous of realization, unknown to their unconscious selves. This does not give them a right to be evil or bad. It is precisely because of this, that an end has to be sought. An end to injustices, of the existence of good and evil wrong and right. I should know this, as they are all me and I desire to realize myself.

Since energy cannot distinguish between good and bad, it resorts to whatever way its power pushes it to. This power has one aim. In the case of individuals on the other hand, they have a mind to differentiate, associate and disassociate the good from the bad. There is no way of justifying any wrongdoing. Realize, admit, and disconnect negative energy. That is the only road to truth.

Do forgive my impertinence dear Soul, but if you are "all that," how can you not realize yourself without putting all these bodies through so much torture of experiencing life for you and enabling you to realize your goal? Is it not a trifle bit too selfish?

So you wish to discriminate between you and me? After all I have ranted and railed about how we have a pact, you and I—now this. Viewed from a point of ignorance, it appears selfish, but that is what makes you so great. You, my noble one, clothed in substance and matter, you climb many a hill and dip down many a valley. You traverse through many meandering lanes until you find your main street, all the while, patiently living a life and going through experience after experience. You endure more of suffering than happiness. For happiness in the world of matter is very fleeting. Its moments can be counted. This is exactly why you do not have to endure. Time is nigh to clothe your self, in new garments. Your nobility fades the moment you allow yourself to be led. You, who are endowed with powers, have deliberately resigned to take what comes your way. In accepting things the way they are. Where is your spirit that fights? That fiery fire of energy that surges and tames the mightiest of energies—Where did you leave it? Have flames of despair extinguished your desire? Have you so demeaned yourselves to occupy the back seat?

Desire? You talk of desire, my dear Soul, most revered one? You who punish us if we as much as breathe the word desire, leave alone aspiring to desire. "Desire begets evil," thus we are told.

These are what your old, decrepit rules say. Do you not see it yellowed over time? Do you not see it frayed and tattered? Look how the ends of the rules curl up and sneer at you. Temptation is the worst evil you say and what you cannot overpower, you condemn! Even if you shriek from the pulpits and tower tops; and call desire an ignominious, vexatious evil, it is what has created you. Even if you twist to the left and twist to the right and shake it all about, and do the boogie-woogie, that's what it's all about.

Desire, the purest most honest prelude to creation; the only revitalizing force. Yet you condemn it. To desire is to empower yourself. To empower is to endow yourself with my attributes. The attributes of an ever full, ever flowing, glowing, luminous sheath of light that neither diminishes nor is extinguished by shedding such radiance. This radiance is that of desire. Desire, not greed, or lust. Desire—the honest truth of creative energy. The driving force behind all actions. But desire with a difference. Let not desire lead you, but be led by You. You are the commander of all powers. To be led by desire is an affront to the self. And how are you going to accomplish this my little one?

How are you going to lead desire?

I shall let you in on another of my secrets. Listen intently for I feel you fading out. Calm the prattle of your mind...now! It does not want you to catch these words. Hush it to silence so you may feel. Awake your senses so they too can hear. Desire is manipulative if you allow it to lead. It leads you to the back alleys of temptations that are illusory and superficial. A bubble, which bursts the moment you, step into it. Heed not to such beguiling words of desire.

When you lead desire, these are the words and thoughts that come to you instantly. The most noble, high, exalted supreme thoughts.

"I desire enlightenment."

"I desire Universal consciousness."

"I desire world peace."

Do they not sound lofty, merely saying it? Think of these words in action and deeds and they become loftier and mightier than the tallest mountain. Feel the magnitude of each syllable of these words and you will concede that you are the power and you have the power. Why do these feelings have so much strength and vitality? Why is it they evoke your deepest sentiments and cause you to hold your head up in pride? Why indeed the effervescent quality of these pure thoughts? Because you are leading and desire is following. Why is desire following? Because your thoughts although desirous, is for the collective good. Your thoughts have included all your copartners of the whole Soul.

What does not include more than the individual's lone enjoyment, is base desire. Such an individual is not even on the bottom rung of the ladder. Hence the word "base." For you are energy that is upward moving. The downward going is for energy on the wane. Energy that is dissipated by self consumed energies. It is energy that has created you and it is energy that destroys you.

Sounds confusing? You should not be confused. You know by now, the useless and the useful energy. You should know now why useless energy is destructive. Unless...unless the useless is transformed. And here is some good news. Transformation is possible, as all energy is moldable. The basest of the base being can be transformed to the highest. The basest metal can be made useful. A swamp can house lotuses and a rose can have thorns. And what goes up does not necessarily have to come down. Gravity is applicable only for energies that are controlled by. Compelled by the properties of matter your body is rooted by gravity, but the spirit within is devoid of such obstructions. It is that by which you can soar limitlessly upward and onward into infinity. But when desire leads you, your power is reduced to a mere whining of, "I want, I need." This is what you ask of desire. You beg of desire. The next time desire takes the lead, tell it, "I AM—all this, and much more. What can you give me? Let me give you instead." And desire will follow you until end.

But what is wrong in getting into the clutches of temptation dear Soul? After all the senses are meant for a purpose. Should we not pamper then? We are sensuous people who revel and luxuriate in pleasure. Those of us, who had no opportunity, make up for lost time when temptation opens its ventilators upon continuous and relentless pounding on its doors. We put the northern star to shame; such is our constancy and consistency at this game of trivial pursuit of the senses. The deprived lot of us consider it a supreme sacrifice and call it, "virtue." The fortunate are those to whom temptation comes voluntarily and embraces with open arms without them having to seek it. Why then should a golden opportunity as this be missed?

Because you have not as yet evolved a way out of it. Do you have the ability to get out of it before temptation gets the better of you? If so, by all means pamper it. When it gets the better of you, leaving vital energy dissipated, your luminosity is reduced. Before you know it you would turn into a shadow. To let anything rule you is the rule of temptation. Be not ruled by anything other than the self, for it knows best.

When you lead desire, your every "I want, I need" becomes a collective whole want and need. You start to think as a whole, with oneness of Soul. Desires become dynamic and an invigorated energy propels it forward and upward. Pockets of spirit energy, pure and radiant bursts forth, illumining the mind and body. With a spring in the gait and passion burning benignly in the eyes, attitude towards everything seen and touched shines undaunted. Undaunted by any obstacles tangible or non-tangible, by any force, good, bad, and ugly, the spirit surges headlong like an arrow that knows its target.

Awareness at a heightened degree snuffs out blankets of ignorance layered under the debris of preconceived notions and ideas. Ideas caused by romantic interludes with desire that held out promises of a different kind and lured its way into the lead role. A role that it usurps by trickery and treachery. Treacherous because it outwits the senses through falsehood and deceit, and makes it think that the "I" is more important than the I AM.

You make it sound almost as if, the senses had a mind of its own.

And so it would appear, for it is tugged at by forces outside your body and the force that is called your mind. Thus the tug and pull, the yes and no and yes again, making you swing like a pendulum back and forth, is the mischief of an unaware state of being.

Enlighten me then on what awareness is. Awareness as I know includes the participation of the senses. A keen observation of what each of the sense perception conveys, is to my knowledge the meaning of awareness.

Sense perception is, as your senses perceive, not as you know. You perceive what your senses convey, and so are led by what and how they lead you. Relegating your own self to a mere observer, you allow your senses to do all the work for you. When are you going to get to work? When your senses fail you?

Consider this scenario for a moment:

If you were born with none of the five senses what would your level of awareness be then? Where would it come from? Would it not have to come from within? Awareness in the truest sense is not perception. Awareness is not knowledge of the "where, why and who," of mundane activities that otherwise occupy your every moment of the day and night. It is the knowledge of the knowing that constitutes awareness. The knowledge that you know, and that you do not have to be led by a sense perception. When you utter the words, "I know," with feeling, your senses play a secondary role. This in itself is important. The moment the idea of, "I want to see, what you want me to see" enters your sense perception, a mirror which is nothing but a mirage, immediately appears before you, obstructing your awareness.

Senses are but windows to the exterior of the immediate you. It is not the exterior that has outlets into you. In other words, you have complete control over what you wish to allow—through which window, and how much of it. Picture your body as a house, with doors, windows and ventilators. By opening your windows to the outside, with no security on the inside, you open yourself to invasions of all and sundry. The all and sundry consists of petty energy forms that disrupt clear thought. This is when perception leads you. With dynamic forces on your side, how and why should desire lead you? Constant waging of war against desire yields not what you ought to desire. Befriend that which intimidates you. In friendship you lose the insecurity caused by needless fears. Applaud it for its tenacity all the while remembering the tenacious will inside of you. Indomitable and magnificent you stand the ultimate of physical manifestation on the material plane. Make me proud of myself that I can look in the mirror of your reflection and bask in its glory.

O desire, thrice desire—I aspire for nothing more, am nothing more and will always be—desire, until my desire is fulfilled.

What of my personal desires, O Soul? Is it so wrong to wish for a little something for myself, to desire a few crumbs now and then, from life? You can take the lion share, but do spare a few crumbs for this poor one.

Oh, you borrowers of the earth, who call yourselves inheritors of the earth! Truly you are store managers. Look how well you bargain for a few morsels. Yes, your whines are the whining of a borrower not the owner, the inheritor. For that, one has to be exalted, and that you seem not. With an outstretched hand you ask for more and more, but you see not that all of this is yours.

Woe! Woe! Pity! What has brought about such depravity that you ask when you are to give? That you seek when you can reveal? Take heed of the cuckoo, which relentlessly and melodiously sings, oblivious to an audience or the lack of it. Where does it get its rhyme and tune? Certainly not from you borrowers! Does it seek rewards for a song well sung? Does the peacock cry out for rewards for the artistry of its footwork? Certainly you cannot give it anything. Yet you ask! This and much more is yours.

This Universe is yours, what of a particle of sand; the oceans are yours, what of a drop of water! See through the eyes of the Universe and your wants seem like a speck of dust. You are not forsaken, you have forsook your awareness, hence the loneliness and depravity.

13

There are no winners or losers
in this game of life; only "becomers."

How have I forsaken my awareness, or rather, how have all of us forsaken awareness? To be unaware is to sleep walk through life. Let me assure you, O Soul, we may be accused of everything except sleep walking during the day. We are aware of all our actions during the day and some parts of the night too. I have never for a moment forsaken my awareness. I am aware of all my actions and non-actions.

Is that right? It does not appear to me to be so. Being aware is being conscious and consciously conducting your actions. Allow me to tell you of how you have forsaken awareness, and this is for all your brethren too, to those whom you keep advocating for along with yourself so loyally and faithfully. That's good. I am pleased with such loyalty. By falling a victim to circumstances, you forsake awareness. Those circumstances and conditions, which seem to permeate your external self, bring about changes in attitude. Circumstance does not present itself to you; you present yourself to it. If you allow a thing to rule, it rules you.

Allowing is "willing." Remember the triangle of thought-attitude-action. These are the constant factors. Constant as the sun that shines—steadfast in achieving your goal, unwavering in attitude despite; who then becomes the victim, if not circumstance itself? So should the stance be, of an attitude well disposed to external misdemeanors of the multitude. Exalted you shall be if through the eyes of the exalted you see. Every other happenstance is rendered trivial when confronted with such a mighty force as the unshakable will. And so you shall remain—despite. Discern every event thereafter, and watch it falling off as the shedding autumn leaves. And so will your awareness heighten and take you to a different level of consciousness. A consciousness that allows you to see truth with the eyes of truth.

Circumvent circumstances with only one thought that of your goal. See it with the eyes of your mind. Thus you devalue circumstance. Not attaching value to it and instead focusing complete attention on something else of a greater importance blows away obstruction creating conditions. Allowing circumstance to dictate your moves amounts to compromising your goal and your highest dream. Once a compromise is sought, there is no end to a series of compromises that follow thereafter. Before you know it, you fall a prey to circumstance and allow yourself to become a victim to it.

What you term as circumstances or conditions contain energy too. Any inkling, a hint of a thought towards its direction, is a go ahead signal to it, and it rushes headlong toward its target, until the target is convinced that to yield to it, is the only alternative. Look from a higher view. Remove yourself away and high up from everything below and what once seemed a tragedy and tragic, will not seem so anymore. To pursue height, and high dreams, thought has to climb high removing itself from the petty monotony of activities below; else it will be twirled in a whirlpool of useless thought.

Thus you lead desires. Thus you lead thought. Thus you lead yourself. So much of importance given to such a trifling like the sensory organs. Tremendous energy exerted towards controlling it has made you go to another extreme of renouncing and removing yourself far from it. That in itself is evidence of its control over you. Have the courage to live with desires, with all of your senses that bring so much wonder, but be not led by it.

The destructive pattern of desires that lead you is very predictable. Energy is predictable. It creates and then destroys its creation. This destruction is not a punishment from god for not absolving yourselves of sin. Neither absconding from desires and the senses, or moderation of the same, the solution to such a destructive pattern. Acceptance and acknowledgment is making peace with it. Holding out a truce flag and simultaneously pursuing a high ideal is relegating it to that secondary position that I stress on insistently and consistently.

If selfish, personal desires are your motivating factors, the non-creative, destructive pattern follows. The percentage of destruction far outweighs creation. If on the other hand, desire for collective good, is the single motivating factor— the driving force of your life, such a pattern is changed. You then mold energy; energy does not mold you. Thereafter every little incident presents itself to you towards the working of such a goal.

Energy is at your disposal to make of it what you will, for your will is in progress for such a venture and overtaking. You might conclude that energy force is selfish, in that it destroys anything that obstructs its pattern. But it is the collective force of all of you, and to think individually amounts to being selfish. It wants what you want, and you want what I want. Although our wants are the same, you have forgotten your wants. Forgotten because of the layers of unsubtle substance you are clothed with. To pierce matter and reach subtlety, mind has to become subtle.

Here is where you play your role—in guiding thought through enhancement of collective, non-mundane attitude of expression, speech and genuine interpretation of pure feeling. Feeling is always pure in every individual; it is the interpretation of it that differs.

Why the differing interpretations O Soul?

Because of differing thought patterns from individual to individual. Basically it boils down to cultural perceptions. Different cultures set individuals minds into a certain pattern of thought formation. Then rigidity sets in. Rigidity of thought pattern stunts thought to attain the vastness that images convey to them through their feelings, which is I. I feel, and I send out images to you. But it is you and your structured mind that interprets what I send to you, in a totally different way. This leads to distortion of the original thought. Then you have an overwhelming urge to specify and label everything that you see, do, and feel. Your need to label everything you see, do and feel leads you to find an exaction of infinity too. How can you limit infinity? It is endless. So too your thought. Because of this urge of precision you desire to find the face of god, and set it up in your laboratories labeling it as "God."

Most of the time, most of you are afraid to think differently and accept something that does not find compatibility with your structured thought pattern. To comprehend something as vast as infinity, your mind has to attain the expansiveness of space. Smallness does not fit in with the bigness. It remains small and diminutive, disappearing in the confines of closed thinking.

Attainment of vastness of thought requires lofty, high above experience of feelings. Merely traversing through space in hot air balloons does not lift the mind higher. Generosity of spirit, and high thinking is encouraged as a means to achieve such expansiveness. Smallness, tightness, rigidity—these are all "down below" thoughts which can never lift you off ground, leave alone understand the necessity to experience the expansiveness of infinity.

But structure is essential for us state loving individuals. We fight with our narrow nationalistic feeling for a homeland. This is our bravest most courageous fight we put up. To live and die protecting one's homeland. Those who do not have one, fight to acquire one. We find the necessity to cling to earth and soil, as our security blanket. We demarcate and differentiate boundaries and regions, people to people. This is what we have done and continue to do so ever since life began. Your message of vastness and expansiveness cannot reach us. We need tangible products.

We love products, commercial and non-commercial. We are commerce minded people. We need proof of everything and that which does not have "solid evidence" to back our theory and concepts, we discard. How are we to believe otherwise what one individual verbalizes or acts on?

Every word spoken, every action acted upon necessitates reason. Reason is the pillow we cushion ourselves on and propel forward with. Without reason, we find ourselves in a maze with no direction. Reason plus purpose equals solution. Life to us is a series of questions and answers, problems and solutions. Those who cannot question or find solutions to problems, fail in this mathematically designed concept called life.

With a structured design like our society that has rules and regulations, rewards and punishments, good and evil, right and wrong and every other polarity of distinction, to experience the "limited," is a lifelong adventure, how then does one experience expansiveness, and why should one, O Soul?

14

Procrastination led many an empire fall.

That's right, why should one experience unless there is a want? There will be a want, when every other method of living life fails. When negative energy intensifies its force on positive energy, positive energy will snap into action. This tautness of forces will give birth to a want. "Want" will snap the elasticity into action. That is the only known method to force. This is your relationship with each other and every other life form on earth. The pressing of bad and good, vibrations and friction between individuals and all other polarities against each other, all seek a release from pressure.

Now I ask a very relevant question to us poor beings that wander in and out of relationships. Like those ships that come to dock for but a night and carry some more passengers going onwards the next morning after dumping, ceremoniously and sometimes unceremoniously, its passengers off the deck. So too do we embark, move on, and some of us less fortunate ones who are not strong emotionally, stagnate collecting moss about us over the years. After getting off one ship we hail the next one soon after. We do this for fear of missing the boat if we do not do so; thus leaving us stranded and marooned on the island until we age like the oak trees, with no one to tie a yellow ribbon. There are many other reasons too for us mortal beings to get in and out of relationships. If, like you said, we enter into relationships to seek a release from pressure, as we are molecules of energy, why should we enter into one and cause friction, heartaches and headaches? We all could lead reclusive lives and avoid friction, thus releasing ourselves.

You could undoubtedly do that. There is no stopping you from doing anything you choose to do, but do this at a conscious level. Your talk of heartaches and headaches arise out of your disassociation from your root, which is your conscious or I.

Dialogue with me and employ me the next time you wish to hail a ship and form a relationship with it. I shall then proceed to give a discourse on the necessity of it until you realize the true idea behind embarking a ship. Let me get a little serious on this subject, for I can feel your quiet agitation over it. Forming a relationship is one method of binding positive force with positive force to counter a negative. Or positive force pressing on negative energy to find a release or negative and negative joining to counter other positive energy. All types of energy have but one goal; to achieve a state of realized form through total destruction or construction. You are not all ships. Some of you are trains and planes too. Not to forget the buses and cars, the bikes and trams and of course the Concorde too. I am not making fun of you. But if you liken yourself to a ship loading and unloading, so shall be your relationships. Every relationship is sacred. Every bond is a loving bond, for all of you are loving Souls. Each of you seeks for a release of pressure, at a conscious level, in order to achieve perfection in evolution. To be able to transform and transmute energy. This is the basic function.

Relegating relationships to mere energy makes it sound cold and unfeeling. There is love and caring involved in relationships. How can energy know what love is?

What makes you think love is bereft of energy? Love contains vibrant, pulsating energy. It stems from the force that you call Soul. Although Soul or force does not have anything to do with it directly. Force generates energy, and energy in turn acts on impetuses and stimulus. Two individuals come together with a deep down knowledge of the actual purpose. Superficially however, they remain unaware of their true intention at the base level. Unless you go within it is not possible to know the why and what, of such a union. Love your "self" that is me, and you will love every other Soul walking on earth. When you do not love yourself, you encounter every problem.

Have a relationship with me, and see how all your relationships become meaningful and not become those ships and planes that you love to travel in. I speak of a love that is powerful, that is me.

I speak of a love powerful and strong,
Not of words rendered meaningless,
In a world of "words."
I look forward to that world,
Which does not whine and wither,
Nor pine and suffer,
Amidst lack luster jargon,
Of misappropriated words.
Into that world I herald love,

Which remains despite,
Petty frivolities of time and tide;
As the ebb and flow of emotions mitigates itself,
And gives rise to the most misused feeling called, "love."
Into such a powerful arena I let love,
Ascend every other trifling desire:
Of hate and greed,
Want and need,
Beyond the material and the non-material,
Above jealousies and rivalries.
I speak of such a love
That all you Souls cherish
Of such a love that would one day manifest itself,
And inherit the cup of immortality.

Yes, my dear Soul, I too look forward to that day. By the way, that is a beautiful poem.

Yes. I derive my inspiration from all of you. An inspiration from your valor in living a life. Love should be powerful and empower an individual and not weaken one.

Now for another crucial question. Does sexual union have anything to do with experiencing the divine? There are so many myths surrounding it and so many people trivializing the myth that it is difficult to know what is true and what is not.

Any physical union is one energy finding compatibility with the other at a lower level. The highest level is at the feeling level where love is experienced even if it does not culminate in a physical union. This is what you call spiritual love. It is the essence of the psychic being residing in an individual that finds compatibility with the other. That's when love finds no reason, or expectations from the other. Experiencing the divine is nothing but experiencing yourself.

Which means you experience what we as individuals experience!

Most definitely! Not as much the physical sensations, for the senses belong to the material world, but at a deeper level. You forget I am the force behind the energy, which acts upon beings.

In other words, you are responsible for the negative and the positive energy to exist. Yet you do not convert everything to positive and put us out of our misery!

I never said I was perfect. You are to aid and assist me and so assist yourself. Would I have asked for assistance if I were perfect? I am all that ever is yet I rely on you to realize complete manifestation. I cannot do without you and you, me. This is the only way I know, through you. I am the force behind every other force of nature. I am the all powerful, yet what is my power without you to appreciate it? I am the exalted, yet if it were not for you, would I have been looked up to? My need for you is more than your need for me. I am within you, around you and everywhere. So are you, within me and around me. We are, because you are the I am. You are god. So awake and smell your god-ness.

Your god-ness—I mean my god-ness, if relationships are meant for like energies or unlike energies to come together, for egg and egg to break, there is no groundbreaking or egg-cracking discoveries made, except relationships that break. Why the hide and seek? Why can we not come to an understanding behind the true reason of forming such alliances?

Because you are engaged in seeing how much each of you get out of each other and whether the other is performing according to one's expectations. Your ego gets in the way of such a realization. It is always false vanity like art that deifies the superficial, the shadows of subtle tones and shades of gray-green colors of lusterless feelings that occupy your energies. Your preoccupation of setting up tiny matchbox houses and shops that you call abodes, is your Becoming—your ultimate and penultimate realization of a relationship. Before you know it, your dream is thrown out of the window, which is open for outside negative energies to act upon your stimulus. Anger, jealousies, greed and every other possible energy consuming and energy-depleting ingredient crawls into your compatibility zone feeding on you. Very soon, production units are set up to manufacture products that boost your ego even further—namely children.

Let me tell you another secret. Your luminosity is robbed and taken by your children. Part of your being is given to them, depleting you of your luminous fibers. Your essence will be on the wane, as the children inherit it. Your dream is diminished and they grow bigger on such strength derived from you. Outwardly and externally you appear every inch of what you once were, but it is the cocoon like shape that is damaged. For you are nothing but an orb of light.

O great Soul, you once said that to even as much as aspire to beget a child is tantamount to weakness of energy unable to contain itself; now you further say that children weaken our luminosity. Yet to have children is supposed to be a sacred tradition...

Says who? Your religious institutions?

But it is a very natural function. To want and desire children, to love and be loved by them, all these are natural instincts!

Undoubtedly it is a very natural function. Every animal and every other species procreate. It is the urge to let out what they cannot contain. The energy builds up to an extent that a spill over is the only other natural way it knows to release the pressure. You have to think of yourselves as particles of force homogenized into a being. For a moment forget the external body.

Consider energy's pressure inside of you, galvanizing you into action, creating the desire to seek an outlet. Consider the sexual desire, as the pressure of anticipation building up and mounting to an extent that the most natural action would be, a spill over, or a desire to seek a way to release the pressure inside.

Shed your vanity for once and really look at yourself, as a big blob of force with a shell, and you will comprehend Matter and other planes of existence.

In other words, sexual desire is a sign of weakness?

No. By all means have a healthy appetite for everything, but understand the truth of the matter. It makes no dent in self-realization, one way or the other. It is your acceptance of truth, which is of paramount importance.

Ego, which is your external self, would like you to believe in what you call the finer aspects of human relationships and sexual unions, but the bottom line remains. The bottomline is that you are a force field. Management or non-management of spirit at different levels is what constitutes and leads you to your goal. Relationships assist in compelling one to look within, for that is what every force sets out to do. The exterior, superficialities however, take prominence and the actual is relegated to the background. Gradually, you move farther away and away from the actual purpose. When you find yourself in a difficult situation in any relationship that is a sign to look deeper from a more "above the human level" angle. When you thus elevate yourself, you begin to look more within and the mystery is revealed.

Feeling a sense of pity or sorrow is not the solution for any situation gone bad or sour for it is not a problem. There has never been a problem, if you would have looked at it from a very stark, realistic angle. Stark realities, however, rob you of your romantic illusions that you create about anything and everything. This is what art and the byproducts of art have led you romantic fools to. To look away from the realities. A deification of illusions (for you find comfort in what does not exist) feeds your vanity, which is of primary concern to you and all of you. How then will any relationship allow you to look any further other than what appears on the outside?

15

Criticism stems from jealousy
Jealousy arises from inadequacy.
Inadequacy takes birth from the inability
of knowing one's inner-self.

O great, knowledgeable one, are you trying to convey the message of taking abuse in order to glean knowledge of ourselves from each other? If use becomes abusive, is one still supposed to continue on and pretend that it is an illusion?

When honesty and truth, however hurtful, are deprived from its rightful position, abuse sets in. You allow abuse; you take abuse for the lack of truth. The truth of facing what is, as opposed to, what you would like it to be. In this, "what you would like it to be," "what you would like to see," lies all the mischief. Here is where you deceive your own self. Lack of confidence to delve deeper than one's imagination, gives rise to such situations.

When "will" is not involved, courage fails. Your question of "why am I here?" should be replaced with "now that I am here." It always is the I Am, not the AM I. That is what is so important about the "I Am" statement. Did I ever at any point tell you to utter "Am I?" Thought is—"I am here." Attitude to that thought should be—"I can do." Action, which follows such an attitude, shall then be— "I will do."

No matter what the situation or predicament, it is how you present yourself to it which is of importance. Passive or active action amounts to action. Passivity to external stimulus and non-reaction is action. Active action involves that which is non-related to reactive thoughts or suggestions. It is not the "why," that has any significance to the self, but the "what," which is significant to your further evolution. Convert the question, "why is it so?" to "what should be done? "Why not this?" to "what if it is this?" Convert, "why me?" to "what am I going to do with me?" The "why" that precedes your every question is the whining of self deceiving, self pity, suffering sensations which, if you pamper, leads you on another road away from the main.

The whats are followed by action, therefore powerful in its very thought. It is power that you seek and power that you thrive on, and only power that will eventually liberate you from ignorance.

Relationships hold the key to a path of self-discovery. Even an abusive relationship opens your eyes to the inside of you, hitherto not revealed. Abuse should not exist, but it is what you make of it which is empowering. Abuse is a form of negation seeking a release with the help of the good, cornering it to an extent of some kind of a breakthrough. The good ultimately, after being pushed to its tether, reacts which is neither beneficial to the good nor the evil, positive or the negative. When good is pushed to its limit, and the elasticity of it can no longer resist pressure, realization of "what is" sinks in and forces it to react or act. The beneficial path is the path of action. When the path of action is taken, it means the "self" has been contacted. The reactive path, is the external stimulus, which is activated.

Now that you consider yourself as a mass of energy with your Soul as the nucleus, (which is a never ending, never depleting reservoir of force) and a being, which is the essence of all experiences that you gather, inherit, learn and digest, ask yourself what it is you want to do with all of these precious treasures. What do you want to mold it to? (Note, the word "want" is used and not wish.)

Would you want your energy to destroy and obstruct and thus annihilate yourself? Or, do you want to adopt the affirmative action of life and seek eternal life, and life at will? Based on such questions, your answers towards your relationships and attitude towards life finds cohesion with every other life force. Such cohesion is the collective conscious energy at work. Whereby you consciously utilize energy to move masses towards a collective purpose. This is your relationship towards every other individual.

Yes, all that is fine, but nowhere have you mentioned about a sexual relationship being beneficial or non-beneficial, necessary or unnecessary.

Because it does not make any difference either way. It is what you make of such an act. It is what you do not make of such an act. Utilization of sexual energy, as any other form of energy, is neither beneficial to you, nor is it non-beneficial to you. Again, it is what you make of it—how you treat it. Do you consider it a sacred act? Do you consider it a playful act to be forgotten later? Is it just a release of energy? Your attitude to-

wards such a thought, for it is a thought first unless it is a suggestion from your external stimulus, is of primary importance. Sexual act based on a suggestion, (not a thought) from stimulus, is reaction.

Once you differentiate between the two, your dilemma will no longer remain so. Your questions trained by a commerce mind, of the benefits and disadvantages will have no place as the flow of ecstasy and feeling of love will make you act in a manner that has no "if" and "but"—only an "is."

What do you mean by, "differentiate between the two?" Do you mean between sexual act and sexual union?

Yes. Because the two are different. A sexual union is action. A sexual act is a reaction to external stimulus. One can perform at a base level without any deep feeling for the other. That constitutes a reaction based on the messages sent by the impulses and external stimuli. A union on the other hand involves a commingling at a deeper, feeling level, and I do not mean emotion but devotion and love. Love is not an emotion, by the way. That love, which stems from an emotion, is fleeting and transitory like those ships you mentioned a while ago.

In other words, you are involved in all actions and not reactions?

Absolutely!

Am I to infer that holds true for sexual action too?

You make such a big deal about it.

But is that not what power is all about? The difference between male and female, and what a vast difference it has been made out to be. Domination of the powerful, does it all not stem from the basic root of sex? It all boils down to that which we all make a big deal about.

Look at the effect a small bodily function has over you. Just hear yourself saying it again! Pay heed to your words and observe the grip and hold you have allowed a function to have over you. Are you not powerful enough to overpower every other suggestion? I am the force behind every energy that you expend, as long as it is an energy, which assists you in getting closer to me and knowing me.

Sexual energy too is yet another way, if you make it a means through which a connection is to be made. For that matter, any other function or duty that may appear mundane, if applied and performed with dedication and devotion, leads you nearer to the truth. Every relationship should draw you inward. Maintain an attitude that would enable the drawing of the mind and the body, inwards.

Inability to sustain any relationship is the inability of such an inward going. A relationship is like a jigsaw puzzle. Once the picture of the puzzle is known, piecing it together takes no effort or time. The Soul is the picture—pieces of the picture are those who you relate to and form relations with. Every relationship so formed is represented by a picture in the mind's eye. Recollect the image of the concerned relationship in question and decipher its representation and relation to you.

Images are the purest form of thought. Give no credence to the dictates of the mind, for the process of analysis and logic rules it. Pay attention to only the image, for it is the most pure form of feeling. Piecing all the images in the mind's eye would eventually enable you to get the big picture of the puzzle—and that is you.

A well-grounded relationship is that which grows together, and does not stagnate. Your experience of each other, with each other and by each other, assists in the growing process. Growth leads to the final culmination of goal pursuit. Pursuit of a goal collectively as opposed to individually is a quicker path to realization. Quicker because one reminds the other and keeps in check the main aim to avoid bypassing the goal.

Thus, fusion of mental and physical bodies, mind with matter, through the subtle element of love emitted by a force that is even more subtle, triggers off consciousness. If a relationship is devoid of fusion it leads to confusion causing an eventual split.

Where does courage come into play in all of this?

Courage and fearlessness are the keys to unlocking the doors to consciousness. Courage to withstand and sustain the test of time and tide, for tests there will be many. To discard your goal at the first seen hurdle or obstacle is fear taking control of your power. Fear of failure, fear of losing, and fear of the unknown causes a disruption in smooth sailing towards an end. Remember that it is what you give importance to that empowers it with such importance. Disrobe it and it will cease to have a hold over you. The inherent desire for one individual to be with the other, at a deep level, is based on selfless desire for the attainment of a common goal. The being inside, (not the Soul) recognizes the vibration of a like-being through past experiences with the other, inside of the body or the outside. At a vibrating level, each other feel waves such as those that cannot be sensed by the common senses. Therefore there is an attraction, or the coming together, of certain individuals with each other.

However, at a superficial level, physical attraction, mental compatibility and compatibility of conveniences for day to day living may be attributed to such a magnetism of individual energy forces to each other. In certain cases, more than one psychic being can occupy the space around the subtle substance of the Soul. When any individual experiences the desire to achieve the desired goal and is open to outside positive energy, beings pervading in space see the opening, and recognizing it as a call, rush in to help with the achievement. Such beings have no per-

sonality or individuality. They remain as beings, either in transition or in seclusion, until such a time when it has recuperated its energies and desires to heed the calling of energies inside of the individuals.

At such times when it finds an entrance into a body, (already living) changes may be observed in the pattern of the concerned individual's activities. Changes are gradual. It slowly weans the body away from the old pattern in so subtle a manner that such a change is mistaken by the human mind as its own mental change.

But succumb not to the dictates of the mind. When you find yourself falling a victim to emotional upheavals, get a grip over your Will or me, for did I not say, I am the one with the hard edge? Will yourself to ignore the various ranges of emotions that rise and fall. Wrap up your ego and put it away. You do not require it. Allow feelings to lead the mind, instead of the other way around, and then observe energy dance according to your tune that is set by your feelings.

The general misconception of the word "feeling" has robbed it off its original meaning. The misconception being, emotional vanity which is misconstrued as sympathy and empathy with waves of compassion sweeping over as a result of self pity. This you call "feelings," when it is not.

When a deep truth coming from nowhere, or so it seems, takes you completely by surprise, causing you to act in a manner not pre-planned by you, go with the flow of such an action. Obstruction of the same through browbeating analysis and internal argument changes the course of direction, in the bargain losing out the original thought.

What has all of this got to do with relationships?

Nothing and yet everything. It is nothing, if you want it to remain as nothing. Question yourself, what it is you want to make of such a relationship, of such a truth, and you will get an answer. Forming relationships and interaction with each other is not the only way to know your inner self. Leading a life of a recluse allows you to avail of the opportunity for a thorough self-examination. For opportunity it is. No other life form enables the study of energy and manifestation of the same. This is your great opportunity that you have given yourself that I have given myself and that I have given you, to give yourself and you to me.

16

Why does one almost always realize
the importance of a thing, subject or object,
only after the thing, subject or object, leaves
one? Because one does not realize
the value of one's own self.

You have just broken the great romantic illusion of a love relationship.

And how did I do this, you creator of romance and illusions?

It does not sound very romantic if love is robbed of its finery and boiled down to the basic, bare truth of the matter regarding a relationship, as you have just done.

Is it because I did not mention flowers and candy and trinkets to go along with the word relationship and love? You smell of expectations, rewards and awards. This is your second hand love that you, award presenting and receiving individuals, give each other. You gloat over an imaginary love be-fooling yourselves into a situation that does not exist. Love, above all expectations, beyond good and evil; compels and impels forces with its mere thought; love, transcends barriers of hate by not recognizing its existence, that is love. Do you have it in your relationships?

Do you form alliances based on such or is it a barter exchange of give and take? You talk of love! What know you of love—creators of hell and heaven, love and hate? You condemn each other into imaginary depths of a bottomless pit called "sin," as a means of punishment to those who transgress rules set by your imagination of love and hate. You profit and loss kingdom seekers, whose ears prick at the drop of a coin! You talk of love! Go back to your relationships that culminate in business transactions.

O pity! How lowly you thus think of yourselves, you, the parent of god. Your heights have thus been reduced to the rubble of the volcanic eruption. Your flight aborted in its wings while eagles dare and you dare not. Why such an error in your internal mechanism? Why is your valor shrouded with a cloak of cowardice that you look not beyond the depths of the clatter of coins. You moneylenders have reduced yourselves to the humps of camels and thus you go around in hump formations, rather than the starry cluster formation. Your materialism and every other "ism" has cast you in a prison with the occasional crumbs thrown at you, for which your eternal gratitude is warranted as a condition for the deliverance of your share. Look how easily you are overpowered.

Those whose generosity spills over, is taken advantage of and generosity mistaken for weakness. Thus you empower yourselves by pushing the truth as far back as possible so it does not hurt on its occasional appearance. You are all aware of the truth yet you pretend you great pretenders, preachers and policy makers. One set of policy and rules for one, and the other set for the others! You pretend for your are all cowards!

O great Soul, stop! I am reeling from this onslaught and barrage of words.

What? Does it hurt you so? Did you think I would impart the truth in pretentiously pristine, pure language that you concocted? Your sweet poison? You pruned, well trimmed poodles! Do you wish to go back to your share of crumbs that a few pieces of metal fetches? I rebuke you into action, until such a time that you do take action. Expectations of each other, from each other, you term love. When such love falls short of expectations set by the standard of your scale, you fall out of love. Oh, how convenient such love truly is! This way, you can go round and around, flit and climb wall to wall to spin some more webs of expectations and trap love in it.

Revenge and vengeance is your morality, for moral sanctions, from one on the other, is the art form perfected for revengeful, vindictive judgements. And sanctions you have got to impose, otherwise how would punishments be enforced? Then you convince yourselves of punishments being a necessary deterrent.

Fanaticism is called religion in your world. Philosophies become dogmas, suffering is called virtue and the good have to bear that label. Evil looks at suffering and prefers to be evil.

Good looks at evil—looks at itself and pines to be evil to avoid the virtue of suffering. Love is give and take—and if there is only a "take," and no "give," it becomes abuse. The abuser abuses and continues to do so. The receiver of abuse out of generosity of the Soul bears the abuse, which is mistaken as a sign of weakness.

The abusers become larger in number, the receivers fewer. The optimist takes stock of the situation and happily pronounces—"I see only what I wish to see," and thus lives a lie. The pessimist looks and says, "of what use—so let me perish."

The idealist artist spins imaginative yarns and romances for a fleeting moment to later turn into a cynic, for lack of appreciation of his art form. Later he is dismissed off by the others as a madman, and packed off into an asylum. "True recognition and appreciation comes only after death." So say your rules. The practicalist adapts a diplomatic stance.

Thus the world, instead of traveling in straight lines, goes round and around—the sun comes up and the stars fade out.

"Oh, is this not wonderful?" cries the imbecile. "God is great to create such polarities of Nature, for who and how would we know what abuse is not, if we are not first abused." This is how all of you justify that which you create and later cannot undo. And you seek rewards for this?

But then if rewards and awards do not exist, there is no incentive for action. We need a little candy for a job well done else why do it at all? We girls need little trinkets too, an occasional diamond or a cruise around the world. When all this is not on the agenda, there is no desire to deliver the goods. So why should I do it, O Soul?

You do it because you are that height which requires no ratification or gratification. You do it because you are the exalted but know not that you are. It is in the "not knowing," which makes you yearn for the lesser. Expectations of what? For what? Is this all not yours? Expectations deprives you of your height, your confidence in the knowledge of the "self," and above all it creates a doubt of your very creation.

You are what you feel. Feel the overflowing Soul within, and expectations vanish. To expect creates a wisp of a doubt and thus jeopardizes action. Result oriented action is a shop keeping attitude. Remember it is the attitude, which is equally important as the thought that works towards an action. An action, which is in perfect alignment with the attitude, thought and feeling, requires no assurances by way of rewards and expectations. An attitude, in perfect harmony with thought, "knows" and hence, "does."

This is how it works. By now you are familiar with the unseen energy and the affect or the non-affect it has on beings and energy on energy. It is the unseen resource that should be utilized. The seen resources exist in physical manifestation, but the unseen, because of its subtle nature, cannot be seen through the naked eye, or through any of the other human senses. But it exists.

Here is how it can be utilized. That, which cannot be touched and experienced through the five human senses, can be experienced through attitude, and attitude alone; until such a time, when mind and body takes a shape of subtlety. When a thought occurs in the mind it means that thought can be implemented; it has the capability of manifestation. If it had no capability, thought would have no place in the mind. It would not sprout up. This has, however to do with thoughts that are action oriented. Reaction oriented thoughts are ideas which sprout under the direction of the senses from the outside to the inside.

Action oriented thoughts come from within and manifests on the outside. Whenever outside energy is allowed inside, without the consultation of the self, reaction occurs. With the attitude of complete knowledge, that which you call self-confidence, without a shadow of doubt of its acceptance or rejection, promulgate and put into action that which is thought of.

To illustrate this with an example; When you start a project A and you require B (a resource) to be available to get to level C; you just create a vacant space for B to fill in—whenever. A long span of time may be covered in the meanwhile, but B does get filled in. This is how energy cooperates. This is your silent, confident communication with energy. The attitude of "whenever" holds the key to manifestation. The "whenever," is confidence recognizing the Soul's capabilities.

As simple as that?

Yes, as simple as that! It only requires your total irreverence towards results and complete dedication and reverence towards action. However, brutal honesty with yourself, is a prerequisite. You cannot fool yourself into thinking you are confident and do not hanker after results, at the same time pine for it deep inside. Eventually it is what you feel inside which is the deciding factor for the success of your action. It is this; "feeling—inside" attitude that does not look for results, for it "knows." You are what you do. It is not your profession in a commerce-related world that decides what you are, and who you are, but your actions that decide who you are.

What is so special in being what you are? You might question thus. It is the state of being and what you are which is the ultimate decision-maker toward your evolutionary step. What people think of who and what you are, is irrelevant. The mob crowd always follows never leads. They criticize those who lead at the slightest fumble. It is their lack of courage, which makes them do so. And an exalted action renders you so and delivers your ideal. Look at the word, "ideal" closely. It says, "I deal." You deal with the idea therefore there is action in it.

Let me tell you, dear one, what constitutes an exalted action:

1. *An action that is motivated by an honest thought, devoid of sole self-interest but of the collective Soul.*
2. *That which seeks not but is sought after, is an exalted action.*
3. *That which fears not heights, for the fear of falling, as it is that height, and those actions that do not succumb to external obstructions or obstacles, with the surety of a positive end.*

All these constitute an exalted action. Such actions do not give rise to justifications or ramifications, as its action is goal oriented and not result oriented.

Most of the time things happen if there is a precedent set, and a set pattern follows, unless the pattern is changed. Energy works in patterns remember it is predictable. At first it is not amenable to change, as various patterns have already been formed. To change it, constant attention to such change and the perseverance of it breaks the mold.

Imagine if you will, particles of energy dancing, 1,1,2. One, one, (up, up) two, (down) 1,1 (up, up).... If you wish to change it to, one, two—one, two, (up, down, up, down) you have to do so constantly, until energy understands the different pattern trying to form, breaks its original mold and reshapes. Imaging is equally important. Forming a mental image, consciously, with the mind's eye, is called "Imaging." A visual always precedes thought. You may not be conscious of it, but there is always an image and then a thought. Conscious retention of the image while, thought is in progress, helps in achieving the target. Almost like a light guiding you. Thought and image send out signals and a pattern is formed regarding that particular thought.

Think of the countless patterns you have already sent forth without your conscious knowledge of it. Think of the colors you have given it, the reds, the blues and the greens. With that, think of the fragrance you have attached to it, for every thought is perfumed by a subtle essence depending upon the quality of the thought. All of these contribute to manifestation of matter. If the end product is contrary to your approval, you wonder what the matter is with it. That's exactly what the "matter" is. Matter-manifestation is dependent on many variables, the chief variable being, your own thought and imaging process. Confused—blurred thinking, contradictory thoughts, and the—back-and-forth swing of "yes" and "no," creates distorted patterns sending wrong signals or right signals, as the case may be, to energy. To go back to the statement on project A with a vacant space left for B to be filled in; with a definite energy pattern, B finds its place and settles in. With an indefinite thought and image, B will never be able to locate its place; hence the permanent vacancy will be experienced. Then you wonder what went wrong. But all the while it is you. Without conscious knowledge of it, it is you who manipulates energy and matter.

You could apply this in human relationships too in a similar manner. Another individual or individuals orbiting pattern, which translates it into a thought form, sending signals receive a pattern set by you. Two individuals with clear pattern formations vibrate to each other's frequency causing homogeneity. This is what you call "understanding." Two or more individuals with similar aspirations and desires, create patterns that are in tune with each other and thus come together as if drawn by a magnet, for magnetization it is, towards the accomplishment of a single goal. This is what you call, "physical and mental chemistry."

Behavior patterns and basic nature of people need not be similar for such an attraction. It is desire that constitutes such an attraction. Desire for attainment of a similar goal. Therefore, physical attraction or desire for the external may last but for a while, if there is a discrepancy in your main goal. Then you wonder what the Matter is with that relationship. Matter formed through such an amalgamation of patterns is not in harmony, hence the disillusionment. A perfect harmony of each other's pattern or structure opens up your own external self to your inner-self. There is an inward going. A relationship that does not contribute to such an inward going is no relationship at all. Lack of enhancement of your own "self," is stagnation leading to saturation.

17

To be honest is easy,
to be dishonest difficult.
Why take the difficult path
when there is an easier one?

Always seek that which enhances your inner self, not the external self. Seek that which brings you closer to me, and does not drag you away from me. Your preoccupation with everything outside of your own body snatches your innermost feeling, leaving you bare and empty. The best relationship you can ever have is with your own self. In so developing a bond, problems cease to be a problem. What you once deemed "a tough nut to crack," opens up like magic. All energy is based on magic; so too with relationships. Magical, because it has the ability of transformation and transmutation.

Everything in physical manifestation is interactive with the same and that which is not materially manifested, too. Every element acts on the other, every substance on the other, matter on energy and energy on matter, one being on the other, and so the list is endless, going right down to a worm. Thus you will find a relationship of everything with one another. There is nothing, which is free from such interplay. Out of such relationships, transformation takes place. A cut apple oxidizes due to its interaction with oxygen transforming its color and properties. A metal tarnishes with its interaction with the atmosphere. All this is the action of energy. The energy in the apple and the energy in the atmosphere interacting with each other thus transforming its properties are simple similes. What you, cannot see, is the apple's effect on energy too. What you see is only the physical object, but the unseen, non-substance is affected too. Such, O little self, is every relationship with the other, and such is the transforming power of one on the other.

But I have heard on the contrary, especially in relationships, that people do not change, they remain who they are and to enter into a relationship with the idea of changing the individual is incorrect.

To impose or force any being or thing into an action that does not willingly act, is to coerce. Coercive policies are those that your institutions and selfish governing bodies resort to. Change and the willingness for such a change has to come from a feeling level. Only then will such a transformation be complete. Such a willingness has to be a voluntary action, something that moves and motivates a being into action. Anything forced is rendered void. Force and compulsion is the activity of energy, which is negative and creates destruction. One being holding loving thoughts of another being, of friends and foes alike however, can infuse a state of willingness into other individuals. This is alchemy at its best. The chemical transformation of love and invocation of love even on one's enemies transforms the individual so holding the thought and the individual about whom such a thought is held.

Love stems from a necessity to give voluntarily. That, which cannot give, does not love. That which gives realizes a necessity for change. It is in such a realization that one realizes the purpose of a relationship, and the circle is complete. This necessity to give, is the abundance of the overflowing of the

Soul, or me. When one feels me, breathes through me, thinks through me, and lives through me, such abundance is experienced. The want or the lack of does not find an inch of space in one who so experiences me. Such a one is an enriched being.

What then, O great one, is the necessity of a relationship when all one has to do is to look within?

To look within; the knowledge that brings an entity to look within, the cause for such an enlightenment is the individual's relationship with the outside of him/her.

What then, O great one, is the necessity of a relationship when all one has to do is to look within?

To look within; the knowledge that brings an entity to look within, the cause for such an enlightenment is the individual's relationship with the outside of him/her. It could be a relationship with an inanimate object too, which would enlighten an individual to take the inward journey, not necessarily with a physical animate being. This is the great opportunity each and every one of you has, to realize your own selves through external means. To squander the opportunity in petty squabbles that deals with vanity and the ego, is a million steps backward from where you have traveled thus far and evolved into mind.

Does that mean I can have a great relationship with my computer?

Mockery is thy second name, O vanity. Know there is life even in an inanimate object. That force which you call Soul occupies every inch of space and non-space. Every brick and stone, every grain of sand, in every particle of dust and garbage do I exist. That which you condemn and discard as "rubbish," too, contains me. It is out of me, on me, and inside of me that all this exists and all that does not exist. Out of everything that exists, there is an origin and out of everything, which does not as yet exist, too, there is an origin. That origin is neither here nor there, but everywhere; it has no beginning or end, it is like a great big vacuum. Chasing such an origin is like a dog chasing its tail.

This is the great big force which all of you are made up of and out of which all of you have come out. This you is me, and I am you.

Yes, yes, you have made that clear before, why then does every hurt exist? Why does suffering have to persist? Why does man go around in circles, without finding a solution? Why does he have to destroy and then construct, only to destroy later? Is there no permanency in either construction or destruction? The ambiguity of philosophies and doctrines—the never ending searches and researches of science; why is there no breakthrough?

Breakthrough, through what? What is it you desire?

A solution to end suffering, pain and disease; of man inflicting harm on himself and others, either through ignorance or wantonly. Most importantly, a desire for physical immortality and the free will to life and death.

> *And so you shall have it. When you commence your becoming. When your upward going halts the constant asking in terms of prayers. (Asking belittles your exalted position) When prayers take form of action; when you begin to "be," that is when thoughts of a different nature occupy the present thoughts. Different, in that, while looking from above, from a height, truth takes a different magnitude and dimension. In order to reach height, one has to be that height, think like height and act in a similar way.*
>
> *Thus you start the process of "becoming a being." God and godliness is nothing but a state of being. An attitude which leads you to such a state. A thought which leads such attitude. A feeling which leads all of the above.*

"If God, is a height yet to be reached who then is god? I was under the impression that you, my Soul, the same that exists in everyone, are God. Now you pronounce God as a state of being. What then are you?"

> *I am what you term "Soul." A force behind all of energy. All of this force and energy is you too. It is you who has created and coined the word God. What is God to you?*

Someone whom I look up to. Some force that is responsible for the existence of all living creatures. An exalted, all knowledgeable being that knows no limits and boundaries. The just and the fair light of truth—this is my concept of God.

Yes, you said it! God is a concept. A concept derived from a deep desire of being it. What you desire you strive for. It is desire and the fervent hope of attaining such a state of perfection, which makes all human beings collective and whole, despite the separateness. It is with such a passion that energy pushes itself towards other energy forms for a breakthrough in a stalemate. The status quo, or stalemate being—the motions of repetitive action and reaction, good and evil. To achieve a condition beyond good and evil—action or reaction, is godliness. A condition to be achieved in a physical form, in a world made of matter, as it is the best of all possible worlds. Thus you condition a free will out of a choiceless, chaotic form of energy, for chaotic it is. Nature unleashes torrents of rainfall in some parts of the world, and leaves it dry to a point of drought in other parts. This is the result of mass energy piling upon each other, against each other in whatever manner and form it possibly can causing to construct and destroy. Unconsciously you have caused such conditions. The right action would then be, to apply conscious thought for every movement and motion, word and deed, to create a condition free, control free environment.

Mind should be cultivated by conscious thought. Conscious thought again is your opening towards me. Every energy form has the same aim and purpose with differing attitudes. Some realize it; the others are enmeshed with mundane, worldly woes, which is an illusion as it is far removed from the reality that you can achieve. So caught up are they with such secondary attitudes that the main street is bypassed and they are lost in the small, narrow lanes.

There is also the tendency among all of you to "accept things the way they are," and "the world as is." This philosophy is a doctrine, which advocates complacency. You are all bodies in motion. Inertia is the antithesis of energy form. Physical inertia results in a sluggish body; mental inertia leads to a dull under developed mind. Movement of every kind is the door to unlocking the potential of energy to its optimum. Any body of water that remains static in one position or place stagnates. Hence the necessity for movement. Forces are always in motion.

Every action is motivated by a preceding action. You are a body that acts, motivated by another body which has set the ball of action in motion. Reaction is counter active and negates action, hence destruction.

Accidents of every form, are reactions, set forth by reactive agencies. Accidental births, accidental deaths, and any form of event are the work of reactions to external stimulus, and not the action of conscious thought. That which is not derived from conscious thought, is not of a constructive nature. Life on earth is no accident. Sounds like a contra-

diction? Hear me out. It is the creation of useful energy with a desire for manifestation. Energy has done its work by creating matter, and matter created mind. It is now left up to the mind, you in other words, to go beyond mind and not create matter, other beings, to break the cycle of energy, matter, energy. When mind goes beyond the creation of matter, it carries energy into a different dimension and evolution. It is the useless energy that creates matter with no thought applied. Thus you have repeated births and deaths.

Since life has been evolved through consciousness, or conscious thought, man is accountable for every action and reaction. Any form of life or any reaction brought forth into the world, has consequences which are manifested later. Conscious thought acts positively, therefore its consequences are calculated for and the possibilities for accidents negated. Accident, is a reaction of force that stems from useless unwanted energy. It is the, "not wanting," which negates and nullifies the purity of any creation. Thus, the byproduct or the outcome of an unwanted and an undesired creation by a product, becomes useless energy.

Energy is again converted into energy. Energy creates matter and matter is again converted to energy. Energy is the constant factor without ever getting destroyed. To channel such energy and purify it to a useful form, "thought" is the only means. Thought is the only means to create a diversion for that which is not wanted, the unwanted, and the undesirable, that which impedes further growth and ultimate evolution. In so doing, the unwanted becomes wanted and thus purifies that which stems from reaction.

Similarly, accidents too can be converted to useful creations, with the knowledge of the futility of such an accidental form, and the conscious effort of conversion of the same, rendering it desirable and "wantable." One want may lead to the door of an non-want, which later becomes the burden you may have to carry. The need and the want to lie or the untruth may leave you with guilt to carry for the rest of a life span. Such a want does not constitute a want. These are wants of an external nature that has to be separated from the desire, which is internalized. The wanting and the non-wanting is nothing but an attitude. Not a perception based attitude, but knowledge based attitude. Life, accidents, death—all of these become unnecessary or necessary depending upon this very attitude towards it. A practical approach however, since you are a practical manifestation of a non-form force, would be the attitude of seeking a purpose. The purpose being, to continue this magnificent manifestation until eternity.

Life and death are not states of being neither is it a state of mind, nor is it an illusion. What an illusion is, is your concept of what being practical is and what being idealistic means. Being idealistic is the practical method applied to life. What you term practical is the easy, short lived way out of a situation that thought and feeling have not been applied to. Thus your highest ideal is the most practical.

Life is the opportunity and death is the end of such an opportunity. An opportunity to achieve your highest ideal. Death is not the final metamorphosis. Death seekers and those who advocate the necessity for death, in order to pursue a better world are illusionists, for no better world exists, save this.

Energy has a habit of propagating itself until an end is achieved. This is why energy will continue to multiply, until the next step for its evolution takes place. Since life is inevitable, a purpose and attaching a purpose to life, becomes necessary. Purpose is seen as a necessity, only if conscious thought is sought. A pathless body, without a goal too, would eventually turn in the direction of "the path." This is inevitable. Means may be many and diverse, some may deviate and digress, but all means lead to one road—one final road of destination. This is the ultimate in evolution.

Relationships, emotional entanglements, professions in a professional life, sedentary life, labor life, or a decadent life, will have to finally take you to such a realization. It is the means that you adopt which is one of ignorance or one of realization. All of the above are but means to a common goal. They remain a means to a positive end, if they are not dogmatic and rigid in nature. Fluidity of thought and expression is the essential of ev-

ery energy force. The moment complacency of attitude sets in, of accepting things the way they are as the best possible way, evolution stops. There is a difference between development and evolution.

Development relates to progress and growth of human life as a human being. Evolution relates to the evolving of a life form in its various stages, until the highest form is achieved. All matter rises in a finished product. The smoke that arises, vapor and steam that water turns into, are all metamorphosis—an end result. Likewise, evolution of a being is something more than just turning into ashes. It has to turn into a super mind. The mind that controls the forces of nature and energy of all forms; this is the super mind.

Since absolute power corrupts in the material world, no power resides absolutely in one force or one institution or one individual. Each and every individual is bestowed with the same amount of power which he calls his will, which is nothing but me, your Soul in action.

"The Universe is a play of energy," you say. Like the smoky taste of cedar in wine—aroma for some, pungent to the others, "it is all a matter of individual perception," you pipe in. Oh how cleverly you conceive ways and means of concealing the truth. In so stating the universe as a playground for energy, you shirk off the responsibility of managing and containing

energy. You, the parent of god, call yourselves children, just so you can play for the rest of your lives and never grow up. To grow up would mean, assuming responsibilities and accountability for actions and reactions, which is beyond your ken. Thus you resort to non-action.

18

There is action even in inaction.
But there is no action in non-action.
Inaction is patience at its wait,
while non-action is the non-attendance
of energy at a time of attendance.

In a world of motion—for every non-action, there is deterioration. For every action, on the other hand, there is a progressive upward motion. Such an upward motion is crucial for evolution. Since actions evolve from thoughts, it is thought that is vital at every step of your life. Every thought "matters." Yes, every thought eventually turns into matter. This is how energy works. It picks up signals of thought, which are not followed by action too, and turns it into matter. They are like consequences, one rolling into the other. Just as consequences enmesh you in a quagmire of rotating energy, thoughts become energy and interact with the outside energy, with one form rubbing against the other, in what you would term a "turbo effect," and causes friction or a productive, positive form, depending upon the thought so thought of.

Life's experiences are not necessarily the result of your thoughts alone. It is the cumulative effect of everyone's thoughts, which finds compatibility with yours. Thus, if for a fleeting moment your attitude takes a downward swing and unintentionally, unconsciously, your mind begins to take on a negative thought pattern, it is sent outside to entangle with similar pattern. Holding your highest thought aloft, like the lotus in a lake of murky waters, with your head in the clouds oblivious to the goings on of everyday routine—it becomes your highest truth.

With your head in the clouds, everything else below appears mundane and boring. Your thought then becomes a dynamic one with a power that sees through any and every petty trifling suggestion that tries to sneak in.

The science of thought or "thoughtology," is the conscious application of mind on energy. When there is a complete and total comprehension of energy and its role in every day life, a method of tackling it is evolved.

Befriending it, the mind, evolves a technique of managing thought and conceiving a game plan, just as one would for any project undertaken. Would you, O dear, vain little self, formulate strategies for a new thought or would you go back to your old law tables?

Will you be able to withstand an onslaught of criticism and alienation, isolation and condemnation, for a teaching that threatens the foundation of rickety religions?

Many have attempted,
Only to succumb out of fear and
desperation,
Of other needs and wants,
And the few times whenever they
withstood,
Old laws, old rules conflicted,
For the fear of being ousted,
The dice of wrong then gambled upon,
In the hope of snuffing out, compressing
and stifling,
The gusty gush of passion sprout.

"Dismay, despair! O woe, O sorrow!"
Thus they droop, and weep,
Lower than the weep of the sweeping,
weeping willows,
Hollow than the sound of hills,
Faster than the wind of mills,
The good—the few and far between,
Snubbed out in a tray of ash,
For the world loves to stoke,
The glowing embers—
Only to go up in smoke,
Not to glow, not now or ever,
On new tablets of law, in old time—forever.

Look at your own anguish, dear Soul. Have you given up on hope? As long as there is a vestige of hope, dreams such as this never die, and as long as there is life, hope never dies. Or is it my mind talking and conveying? It is difficult anymore to know who or what is interspersed by which.

This is what is experienced when consciousness pervades every pore of your being. Your mind, senses and all other aspects of thinking is open and mingles with the consciousness. That which had hitherto been cohabiting without actual contact with each other with the mind assuming an identity of its own; it now realizes and recognizes another force. Cognition by the mind of the soul, is mind's way of yielding and relinquishing control. The relevance of differentiation of mind, soul and senses then becomes irrelevant, as every action taken thereof, is for the highest good.

Time, unlike tide, does wait patiently at your door. Gently does it approach and soft as the feet of a dove it settles upon space on an imaginary shelf—waiting. Waiting with a hope in its seconds and a longing in its hours, as grandfather clock ticks away his tock, tick-tock-tick-tock. Unruffled and undisturbed by the flurry of useless energy causing tidal waves to lap up the ocean of humanity in its wicked embrace, it waits. Waits until such a time when all of consciousness releases it from its tedious yoke.

It is an interesting study, the science of thought. Start observing what thought leads to what action and you will get the picture.

But that is what philosophy does. Where is the difference between thought and the analysis of thought? Does it all not boil down to the same sediment residue?

What you call, "philosophy," deals with the thinking process of thought. Where as thought as a science deals with the quantum of energy released by each individual thought; the re-leasing of energy to you in exchange of what you lease out as thought into space. So what you send forth comes back twice fold. But then again, you are only released or re-leased. Your lease terminates when you "realize." Until then you are a tenant in the hold of your energy lord.

When the amount of energy is calculated in terms of force, or quantity, each thought weighs that amount. If you create boulder like energy, the velocity and speed with which it comes back at you is like a ton of brick hitting you. Then you wonder why? What weighs less and what is heavy? Is heavy better than light?

Remember one rule, the greatest of things comes as a light feather touch, as a whisper, as soft and gentle as a dewdrop. The skein of thought should be as light as lace. To be entangled with the frivolities of time and petty emotions, hampers free movement of thought.

So what then shall we think about? You have ruled out almost all avenues of thought.

All but one, and in that one there is diversity and divinity in such a diversity. The one thought, which embodies the all, is of magnitude, of love. It is love and love alone which uplifts. Thoughts that bind you, are those that arise out of fear. Possession, greed, vengeance, destruction, harm, all arise from fear of the unknown. When you are that "known," what then is there to fear? Eliminate fear, and thoughts soar; of generous feeling to one and all, to wish well despite it all and most of all, not to be affected by the reactions of anyone. Marching bands of distant sands come and go without as much as a cursory glance at what might be if only they befriended time.

Time is always looked at as the enemy, racing against, competing with, and finally condemning it to damnation when death waits at the door and time blamed for everything. Yet it waits with knowledge brought on the wings of hope, that someday its illusion will be shattered and reality experienced.

You are digressing, O great one. We were talking about the science of thought.

Thought and time go together. Did you ever realize how you lose track of time when lost in thought? Time holds no great significance when thought takes predominance. Cultivate thought as you would a garden. Weed out the negative and follow its every movement and trail.

Form a graph in the mind's eye. As a thought takes you one notch lower or higher, graph it. At the end of the day, calculate the graphics. You will see a pattern beginning to form. For every notch lower, deduct a point and for every higher rise, add one. Count your points at the end of the day. Follow this routine every day, and collect your points. Match your thoughts with actions, and deduct two points for every lowly act, and one point for that which is uplifting.

Why the discrepancy? There are two points deducted for every one point added!

Because, it is easy to lower the consciousness to a base level, and twice as difficult to raise it up. It requires tremendous will of energy to lift it upwards. Observe how easily an outside suggestion that floats on the breeze can sway you, and how your thought takes on a lower dimension, without your conscious awareness. Become aware, and mitigate those thoughts that drag you down. That is not so easy. It requires practice and a certain way of looking at things, a certain attitude, which does not come to you on a platter. You have to work for it. You have to earn every thought that surges upwards—for that one point. Give yourself colors for every one point added, like medals for bravery. The colors of the rainbow are your medals. The highest medal, is the color purple. For every point deducted mark a dull gray blotch. Next take a look at the pattern of colors so formed.

This is how you weave your own blanket of sky with its myriad colors. Every color has significance as the numbers do. The reds, the greens, the browns and the blues, so you spin exquisite yarns in your mind. This is important, as these are the patterns and graphics, which follow you in cluster form, subtle and unnoticeable they may be, but they act on your every mood swing and action. Numbers and symbols, like images, is me talking to you.

Whenever a number crops up in your head quite suddenly, in your sleeping moments or the waking hours, take note of it. Decipher it, as the Soul is conveying something to you. The most crucial number is number seven and all derivations of the same. These are all your grades towards ascension. From the base to the highest. The base or the root number is as important as the highest, as it is the foundation of all numbers.

Every time there is a drop in thought, where a thought has fallen into the clutches of perception, there is a drop in the rise of the spirit or energy. Perception borne thought differs from conscious borne thought. It is easily detectable. I have already mentioned it. Avoid getting enmeshed in the plethora of feelings that perceptions lay out in front of you. They are illusory in nature, in so much, the objects you perceive outside of your immediate self, are not real.

Your senses are affected by another energy that makes you look at them that way. The only way to avoid this is to keep the energy level of thoughts constantly upward, and upward moving; almost like bouncing a basketball on your knees, to prevent it from falling to the ground.

If, as you say, perceptions lend an illusive mask to the objects so perceived, how can every individual see an object in the same way? The basic, inherent characteristics like color, everyone views shape and size of any given object in the same dimensions. It sounds as though there is a colored glass, so subtle in nature as cannot be seen, a sort of a fine film or layer that hangs like a cloud, between us individuals and the outside objects.

Yes, you are all encased in a bubble, with the objects outside of your immediate self. When the conscious is evoked, this bubble bursts, the film slowly peels off revealing reality. This bubble can only be burst, unveiled and exposed with mass conscious thought. Some of you are aware of this truth, but the mere knowledge of it is not sufficient. As with everything in this world, it is what you do with such knowledge that is important.

Application of such a truth leads to awareness. An awareness beyond what the five senses can convey. A stark, bare all, revealing reality. The science of thought, or the systematic approach to thought should lead you to energy management, and so lead you to towards your goal.

It somehow deprives life of its finer points, if thought were to be systematized and applied in all walks of life, don't you think O Soul?

Such an emotion is the result of the untruth that you have been living. Under the garb of art, you create vanity, and so remove yourselves further away from what you are supposed to get closer to. Under the misguided notion of a fairy tale romance of life, you create some more illusions, further veiling the already veiled Soul. But be prepared for death as an eventual end if you prefer to live in an illusory world. You are all immortal beings; therefore immortal thoughts should and must occupy the mind.

When two or more minds come together with a single goal, it becomes a common thought. A common, single thought of mass people has a resonant resounding effect that carries through space like lightning. It is only thought that travels faster than the speed of light. That is why, next time you think a thought, think with care, for once discharged it wastes no time. It shoots out into space, before you have the opportunity to take it back. Almost like words. With words, you have a chance to apologize and take them back, although its effects will still be there. But with thought, that opportunity is not given. Therefore be responsible for your thoughts.

Laxity and carelessness leads to many a misadventure of the spirit. Maturity is not required to acquire this level of understanding. Simplicity of mind leads to the opening of the heart to the consciousness. It is in the most simple that the most complicated is solved.

19

Lament not on what you have not done.
Re-cognize (recognize) that which
you "will" to do.

What is simplicity of mind? Is it the same as being a simpleton and a fool?

You pronounce the word "fool" in a derogatory manner. A fool has no worries; everything to him is a wondrous adventure. With one leg perched at the edge of the cliff, oblivious to the dangers ahead, he carries on, on his journey called life. This is the attitude one should adopt. A simple mind is easier to mold than one, which is caught up with the detailed latticework that sense perceptions lace it with. While your sense perceptions convey one thing, your conscious within conveys another message. A simple mind finds it easy to decipher which is which, while the mind that is complicated, finds itself in a quagmire of doubts battling between illusions and realities all his life. It all the more reiterates your necessity of letting perceptions guide you from the inside out. This is how the process of thought should evolve, from the inside out and not the other way around. You should not be caused to think. Thought automatically comes from within. Being caused to think carries the illusion and its effect a step further, for thought thinks not, it just "does."

Newton would not have done any thinking had the falling apple not inspired him. The apple in so falling caused him to think.

Not so! Newton, was in seclusion at the time he thought of his theory. That seclusion helped him go inward. Unknown to him, (according to the world, but known to him) he made contact with his conscience. The idea of inspiration therefore was not in the apple falling from the tree, but his own power, which caused the apple to fall and so acted as an agent to what he already knew.

Here, it was his inward-going while in seclusion, which is the source of his theories. Apples and oranges falling from the tree did not have any relevance to him or anyone until that time, and would not have had any significance either had it not been for that exclusive time Newton gave to himself.

Quietude, both external and internal, is essential for such a contact with the inside. An extra sense of awareness is developed in the atmosphere of quietude. Especially mental quietude where you stop the incessant, internal dialogue or chatter of the mind. An illuminating thought or idea springs up and messages are conveyed, through no fixed form as such. It is just a feeling as you are experiencing right now.

Right! You, were telling me about Newton, the apple and thought flowing from inward...

Don't get impatient. You heard me reprimanding you for your transgressions, and now bear with me for some digressions. Unlearn the thought process. Un-think that which has become internalized in you. Undo what perceptions have superimposed upon you. In so doing, that power, which the object held causing you to think, is undone with you retaining the power of thought.

Here is how it works. Objects and everything external should not "cause" you to think. If this happens, the power vested in you, is automatically transferred on to the object in view. On the other hand, projecting from the inside to the outside shatters all illusions any external objects may hold for you, and also retaining your power within you. The objective here, is the same principle of "giving" instead of "taking." Therein lies your power.

In the case of the reverse, wherein an object is the cause of your thought process, the external object holds sway over all of your emotions and mind, molding it according to the illusion it holds. This is because you are "taking" from the object, not "giving." The more you give the more power and control is retained within you. Control of your "self," over the external whereby, you are the cause, and not the consequence of such a thought. You cause thought, you cause the world, you are the creator, and this admission is your ultimate power.

That, which undermines or weakens the pure energy within, is not a pure thought. Since thought is dynamic and powerful, it cannot be relegated to the external. The surging spirit within has to rise and burst forth like an illumined bulb for thought to emerge from within. The beauty of nature no doubt is a spectacle to behold, but it is not the cause, it is a mere consequence of your thought.

To allow nature and every beautiful and non-beautiful object to hold you in its grip is subjecting your "self," to second place. Look at it through the eyes of the Soul, and you will see what Nature is in reality.

The adage, "appearances are deceptive" holds true. Deception caused by that which appears "to be," while it is not. When a "thing" or an emotion is not given the dominant position of a "cause," it ceases to dominate.

Similarly:

1. *When anger does not cause you to behave in an untoward manner.*
2, *When the reactions of some does not cause you to react to it, and*
3. *When an object does not cause you to think.*

It is then that you see right through the object rendering it devoid of a cause; you become the most supreme thought. You hold the absolute power.

Dwell not on trifling, petty, energy consuming ideas. Waste not this opportunity of life you have given yourself. Destroy not that which has taken you thus far towards realization. Everything else is valueless. Thought, and thought alone is your vehicle to immortality, taking you to a new consciousness.

So listen up, O ears,
For we want to hear,
The rumble and the tinkle,
Of which the conscience within speaks
And not what you "will" us to hear.
Wise up, O eyes
For we want to see
What our Souls can feel
And not what you wish for us to see.
Hush, little mind—
What art thou in comparison to the "self" in each of us?
O little vain self, that is the "I"—we bid thee sleep.
O heart, flutter not helplessly,
For thou sheltereth that "will,"
The great strength which hast many a
Mountain moved,
Be the force, before that "will."
And when you talk, O great big self,
You shall rumble like thunder,
For the voice of truth is loud and clear,
And not as a mousy squeak—feebly voicing,
Drowning in the ocean of fluster.
When you move, you shall glide,
Fly with unimagined velocity
Into unspeakable distances,
For the spirit likes to glide and flow,
Fluid, liquid—unimpeachable—forever
Flowing, forever glowing.

O great Soul, you once said, "Man is the result of the inability of energy to contain itself," thus reducing all our notions of life and the great big plan the architect had drawn up for us.

Is it so difficult for you to digest energy? For you digest it every second, even as you breath. Life giving energy, that is air, life giving energy that is food, life giving energy that is water, all this is energy. Forever moving, changing and ever in motion, energy commands and obeys, conquers and surrenders. Surrendering of energy to its inability to keep its force within itself results in its splitting into two or more parts. This is how life forms. But it is recognition of consciousness with the application of mind that differentiates man from other life beings, all consisting similar energy.

How is this recognition of consciousness possible? To understand, you have to become clear on what consciousness is to begin with. You have given yourself the opportunity to experience energy and understand it. Every opportunity is a precious one—if you utilize it. Did you ever wonder why upon reading a particular thought or listening to some uttered words, it triggers off another thought in you? You may think your thought to be unrelated, but it is not, as every energy has a relationship with each other. The next time you meet another individual or read some thought somewhere, observe how your thought takes on a different dimension.

It would appear different to you, but is a branch of the same thought. Did you ever wonder how a certain individual inspires you into a certain form of action? How a poem is written or a story written? It is your energy mixing with the energy of the concerned individual, which results in such a manifestation. Every thought manifests eventually into some kind of physical form.

O Soul, we householders and people with careers and responsibilities do not have the time or the energy to sit and ponder about "energy" and its uses. We expend all of our physical energy on the sustenance of our relationships, rearing of our children and providing a livelihood for ourselves and our future generations. This has been an age-old practice which we, as the inheritors of traditions and conventions handed down by our forefathers, (and foremothers) continue on faithfully. Anything exercised on the contrary, results in us alienating ourselves from those who adhere to such practices. It is out of such a fear that we mortals, fearing the ticking away of the biological and physiological clocks, rush on to the bandwagon that carries the mob.

Did I not tell you, my dear little self, that it is fear that leads to all your decision-making processes? Why the fear? Fear of what and from what? Why the insecurity? Why such destitution? Remember that desperation leads to many an unwanted turn. Again, you attract the on-rush of useless energy at such times of desperation.

You assume that it is important to be a householder, to have a career, to have responsibilities. You choose them consciously or unconsciously. If you only pause to listen to your conscience and be guided, you would consciously apply energy and thus unlock mysteries of the physical world.

Conscious energy is everywhere, occupying every inch, every nook and cranny. It is immutable and immovable. Soul force exists everywhere, in a needle and a haystack too. It is neither in nor above, neither outside nor below, but just "there." Awareness of consciousness or conscious awareness is the utilization of this force by the mind.

There are two levels of awareness. (1) An awareness created by perceptions, and (2) conscious awareness. These two awareness are distinct. One creates illusions; the other destroys the illusion and exposes the truth. Conscious energy is constructive, perceptive energy is most of the times misleading, creating doubts in the most confident of minds, about their ideas and concepts.

Conscious thought works towards a common goal while perception-based thought is almost always individualistic in nature. This disparity is because in one, knowledge is inherent, in the other, knowledge is deduced with the utilization of more than one factor. You should know by now which is which. The one with inherent knowledge is conscious energy. Knowledge based on deductions is not always reliable, as the element of doubt will always persist. Element of doubt will exist when a deep-rooted knowledge of the existence of another more authentic and reality based knowledge, lurks in the corner of the mind. How many times have you not doubted the outcome of an action? How many hours have you not dwelt on regrets? Consciousness knows no regrets. Conscious awareness directs and guides and finally leads to the desired goal. Actions ensuing from such awareness are positive affirmations of life.

Follow the route of thought with doggedness, not losing sight of it. The moment you see a slip and a little digression into the narrow lanes, pull it back on the main road. Constant practice of the same allows the mind to follow a pattern of thought, which finally acts as the key to unlock conscious force. Unlocking the conscious force makes the energy level rise up.

Before you question me, let me explain it to you. There are two levels of energy in every physical, living being. The perceptive energy or perception based thoughts, occupy the lower energy level, which is where all living creatures' level is placed. The coveted upper level is occupied by the energy of conscious force. When any thought finds compatibility with an outside thought of similar properties, the energy level climbs to the upper level.

Energy gets excited, (as there is a filament of lower energy climbing to a high level) with this sudden rush from a lower level to a higher level, and emits rays of light from the body. This is not visible to the naked eye, but these rays of light are of immense magni-

tude. Such a charged energy when discharged out of the body takes on another form of energy.

Although there is enough of such supercharged energy that has the capability of breaking space that has been frozen by time, and a new enlightenment made possible to all life forms, the energy of mass consciousness is essential. The mass conscious thought of beings is more powerful than a handful of conscious thinkers.

Think of the amount of energy that mass people can generate when they dwell on a single thought, at the same time. The force is tremendous. The energy exuded is stupendous. Energy therefore equals mass consciousness. Any mass congregation with a single goal achieves much more than a single individual. Energy emitted by all beings in such a gathering spirals upwards, as one point of energy connects with the other and links it up to form a common goal. This holds good for any goal, be it positive or negative.

History is proof in showing this possibility. In the negative sense, Adolf Hitler achieved this feat. A destructive pattern, however, is short-termed, as it does not lead to the final realization. Short termed because it is in direct opposition to the affirmation called life. Destructive energy and work carried on through the use of destructive force is energy trying to get a breakthrough. There has to be enough good, positive energy emitted for egg to crack on egg resulting in an outcome that conscious force wills all the time.

Energy as mentioned before, has a habit of manifesting itself, transforming and transmuting all the time. Therefore it has the attributes of alchemy and magic to every form of energy. And it is magical because of its properties of pliability. But energy is predictable and forms in a pattern that it "knows" best. The energy that manifested in the form of Adolf Hitler knows no better than to form a being and wait for manifestation in, if not a similar form, a kind of destructive energy. This is why energy can be predicted. Once a pattern is formed, it sticks to its geometric formation, until and unless changed to another pattern. This is where "magic" comes into play. Conscious awareness applied to this knowledge, and conscious application of thought and mind to another conscious transformation, involves a magical process.

Dear Soul, why should energy manifest itself in a negative material form to begin with? Why do such polarities exist?

And they will continue to prevail as long as there is compulsion. For the total amalgamation of negative and positive to one constructive, perfect form, compulsion and coercion should not be applied. Anything forced yields to the creation of such contradictions. Did I not convey that energy does not have a mind? It is left to you to utilize the mind and create perfection without coercion.

How is that done?

You can do this by constantly bypassing the existing contradictions and dwelling on the imaging of loving thoughts on living beings. You are not doing anyone a favor in so being, except your own self. Energy tricks you into turning your most loving moment and thought into one of doubt and hate and eventual loss of faith in your own "self," by creating another moment that would negate the positive. Ignore it and do not succumb to it. Keep that loving moment aloft, above and beyond the reach of such petty energy.

Such an energy of love so transcended yields a pocket full of positive ions, which spiral into space, mingling with like energy. Thus you accumulate the "good."

Please forgive me for my ignorance, but how does one transform the bad energy of one individual to good when you just said that coercive policies and tactics should not be applied?

By visualizing, dear one. In so filling your own being with thoughts of love, you fill yourself with light. You are all beings of light. You grow luminous with every thought of love. Those whose energy is on the wane are those individuals who do not have enough light because of lack of love. By "energy on the wane" I do not mean physical energy, but energy of spirit. If you recognize those individuals whose energy is so depleted, all you have to do is send images of light floating on a cloud of pink to the concerned individual. The more number of individuals you hold in the images of your mind in such a column of light, the more the magical transformation of base to gold, undone to done, imperfect to perfect, without any coercive policies adopted.

But what if the concerned individual is not receptive?

You are forgetting the A B C's of consciousness and Soul force. Every being has at the root level the same consciousness. If you, as a thinking and a feeling being get in contact with me, as you are doing now, you are indirectly getting in touch with the overall consciousness prevailing in everyone. Thus, if each individual gets connected with the conscious force or the conscience within himself/herself, he/she is automatically connected to every other being. Let me explain before you jump up with your questions. But before that, there is something more about energy that you ought to know.

And what is that?

That heat is energy and energy heat, you are aware of. Part of that energy is consciousness too, is something your physicist Joule while exploring about heat and energy, remotely came close to.

I have not the remotest clue as to who Joule is. I am afraid my knowledge of physics and science in general is very limited. Please enlighten me. First of all dear Soul, how is it that you know this without me actually knowing all of this?

That is what consciousness or Soul is all about. What I am all about. And what you are all about too. Allow me to explain what our friend Joule the physicist who theorized on heat and energy came up with. Joule's principle of heat and conversion of heat explained about the conversion of heat into energy. He called this potential energy, kinetic energy and internal molecular energy. He observed that the temperature of the waterfall at the top differed from that at the bottom. He called the energy at the top "potential," which then gets converted to "kinetic" on its way down, and on reaching the bottom gets internalized or "becomes" internal molecular energy.

I notice your parenthetical word "becomes." Are you trying to tell me that all energy "becomes" into something?

By Jove you've got it! Or should I say "Eureka?" Now back to what I am trying to convey to you. All that there "is" is consciousness. All of consciousness is energy, yes even the bad energy. But it becomes "bad" if it has lost contact with consciousness. Thus you see good even in the bad. There is potential consciousness outside of you and every living being. That which has the potential to "become." Energy or consciousness in the process or on its way to getting internalized transforms to kinetic consciousness and is later converted to internal molecular consciousness at the birth of a being, human, animal and plant. Thus there is a constant interaction of potential and internal consciousness.

How is it so? Once consciousness gets internalized, where is the necessity for it to become into something else?

But that is exactly where it has stopped at, and that has limited its potential. That is what has limited me inside of you. I have become internalized and sitting pretty twiddling my thumbs and cooling my heels, painting my nails and those on my feet.

Now you are making fun of me!

Where has your sense of humor gone, my little self? Have a few laughs now and then. Ever viewed two warring nations or a pack of men and women fighting and squabbling like petty children? Watch them from afar and you will notice the humor in it, right to the gory details of blood gushing forth from wounds inflicted upon each other. It is funny because of the nature of the fight. Like children fighting for toys. View it through the eyes of consciousness and you will find it rib tickling funny. And speaking of nature, personal nature as well as characteristics of an individual, the general environment that is termed "Nature" and consciousness is one and the same. The basic nature remains the same, with consciousness reigning supreme.

Do we as human beings have a duty towards you or consciousness? Your continuous reminder of "becoming" makes me aware of a sense of duty towards you and myself?

There is no duty that you "will" not want. Your ultimate duty is towards the "self"—yourself. Plug into the socket of general consciousness and watch it trickle in, first drop by drop and then in a steady stream. Every breath taken is consciousness breathed in. As you exhale, consciousness is breathed out. Did you ever observe your thought process during the inhalation and exhalation? Take notice of it the next time you breathe in and out. With every breath taken, the foremost thought attracts that part of energy which consciousness brings in. A positive, loving thought would bring in positive energy, like perfumed breeze. And when you exhale, breathe out the same so the atmosphere would be charged with positive energy.

All such charged energy spiral upwards. Energy always has a spiral form. From a dot, a grain—a drop, to a wave, it twirls upward and outward. Insidious energy carrying waves of hate and destruction obfuscates a mind that lacks awareness of "awareness."

Do you mean there are two types of awareness? And here I am blissfully soaking in your every "feeling" contented with your lack of concepts and terminology unlike us who get our Ph.Ds and doctorates for the concoction and creation of different concepts, terms and theories!

Patience! Have patience dear self. All of consciousness is awareness but not all of awareness is conscious thought applied. Still confused? That is how all of you have misunderstood and undermined actual "awareness." Perceptive awareness is all you know of. You forget there is an actual awareness within you, which does not require the aid of perceptions. Your awareness should be, "attention given to the here and now." In other words your immediate instinct. I cannot emphasize enough on that one word, "instinct." Perceptive awareness is, being conscious of the external, "the there and then." But before the external gets manifested, there is the actual awareness or consciousness, or me, that can either change such manifestations through your conscious application of me or, let perceptions guide such manifestations.

Perception based awareness and actions based on them yield results beyond control. Do you want to know why such transformations are uncontrollable?

Yes I do.

Material manifestations based on perceptive awareness can never be controlled. To a certain extent you may have control, but that would again lead to some more unseen and unforeseen conditions which you have to grapple with later. Here is why. Because that which is "acquired" is lost. That which already "is" remains. That which already "is" is me. I remain—despite.

The first requirement of such an acquisition or any other type of acquisition is the expenditure of what is required to acquire from the outside. The expenditure of internal energy. Such expenditure involves "unconscious" thoughts and actions. Such actions would predictably result in "the good, the bad and the ugly." Awareness of consciousness on the other hand, enables you to plug into the general consciousness and thus communicate with the Nature and the nature of beings as well as non-beings.

Every stick, stone and rubble possesses consciousness. Communicate with it on a conscious level and watch it communicate with you on a feeling level. This is how each of you can get connected to one other without actual verbal communication, because all of you are connected at the root level, as mentioned before. You branch out as trees growing outward whichever way the wind blows and takes you, losing touch with your roots and being disconnected from each other.

You then set up cable wires and computers to communicate on a superficial level. How then are you ever going to take control?

Here is yet another secret. There are unseen wires connecting all of you.

Is that a joke, dear Soul?

I am absolutely serious. Just get conscious and you will begin to tap those wires. Don't get even when you are mad about someone or something, "just get conscious." Coming back to the potential conscious and kinetic conscious—there is a profound and a deep relationship between me, and the outside, potential consciousness. Although it is one and the same, there is a difference in that, you get to apply your mind and use this internal consciousness. In so doing, energy is converted all the time you use me. For every conscientious conscious act, columns of potential energy is converted to—hold your breath...

Oh wait, I think I know the answer. Kinetic and then internal energy?

If that were the case, then the earth would indeed be overburdened.

But why and how?

That would then mean the birth of some more beings and you would not want that. There is another way of converting energy to another form other than internal energy, and that is...

God force?

Hurrah! Yes, thrice yes!

Please explain how this can be accomplished in terms that does not come under physics or any other science.

Here is how it can be accomplished. Once it is seriously established in you that thought accumulates energy and creates non-substance entities, you become aware of your every whisker of a thought trying to sneak in. Conscious force exists, and will continue to exist, whether or not energy manifests itself on the physical plane, or whether space, which is frozen in time, will be shattered into fragments of ice and melt away all illusions.

You, however, have been given the opportunity to break the ice and decode the secret to eternity. To dwell on the useless and throw away such an opportunity on petty, frivolous little gains which does not last, is a wasted opportunity. Now getting back to the process of each individual getting connected to each other, the internalized energy force within each other is the same. If "A" connects with this internalized Soul force within him/her, he/she gets connected with the general, overall Soul force residing in "B." If "B" were to connect to his/her Soul too, he/she would be able to send forth a silent transmission and receive one without any direct contact by way of speech. Thus you begin the process of "becoming." All that is required is to silence the mind and send waves of light through images held in the mind's eye. Images of individuals whom you come in contact with and have done so far and will do in future too. Negate any negative image that comes to the mind's eye. That is just the trick of the mischievous energy. Blot it out by filling yourself with all the love and send forth columns of loving feeling. This also involves science. Yes, everything that you have and experience on the material, physical realm, is a science.

And pray how can love be defined as a science?

Love is a feeling. Like it was mentioned before, not an emotion but a deep down feeling, that relates to energy. Whenever the feeling of love is activated, an expansiveness is experienced internally. Your molecules expand and consciousness is heightened. Thus you release pockets of the absolute pure energy. An energy that assists the other energy in transforming the bad to the good.

Let us go back to the energy of Hitler.

What do you want to know about it that you do not already know?

Why was Hitler so far removed from this collective consciousness, yet have such a tremendous impact on the masses, irrespective of the thinking intellect or the non-thinking intelligentsia, irrespective of genders and irrespective of all aspects of love? Does that then mean destructive energy is more powerful than positive, good energy and feeling of love?

The answer to your first part of the question, the mass intelligentsia is just that, "mass." A herd that refuses to "feel" for themselves and prefer to be satellites to another orbiting sun, even if it means that the sun would ultimately scorch it to cinders. A mass that does not realize and recognize its own luminosity, its own sun within. Those individuals who keep their doors open for any and every type of energy to enter into them, are all the more susceptible to destructive molecules. Those little molecules quivering with delightful anticipation of gaining entrance into new territories to wreak destruction, seek individuals who are open minded to such thoughts. Wobbling and hobbling, it hovers around, playing with the sense perceptions for easy access. Therefore conscious awareness becomes all the more necessary.

Now to answer the second part of your question, energy in itself is powerful whether positive or negative. It is the application of it, which determines its ultimate power. Proper and improper utilization is what leads to construction and destruction. Short-term goals are very appealing as they only highlight the superficial. The superfluous minds that cannot see beyond and the above, take in what meets the eye and what hits the sound waves. Taking that to be the ultimate truth and the ultimate good, they convince themselves into a false reality by suppressing the internal voice and subjugating it into silence. The fear of truth is so great that the feeble voice of untruth appears to be more resounding and appealing. Why does this fear persist? I shall tell you why. Because of the fear of losing your external shell, which again is nothing but an accumulation of perceptions.

Your constant habit of scurrying back to those concepts and terms that you constantly give and label as "good and evil" will continue until such a time, as this fear is prevalent. It is you and all of you who attach that importance to hate and destruction. Constructive thought never dwells on the negative even if the negative exists. If, for example, a matter "X" has manifested with negative attributes, conscious application of thought will transform the negative to the positive, just as the basest metal is transformed to gold.

If a matter called "A" recognizes that matter "X" has destructive attributes, "A" can, with the power of such magical knowledge of transformation and transmutation, convert base energy to perfect energy form. But again, without any coercion. It is not the "why" that is important, but the "what." The attitude of, "now that I am here what can I do," not, "why am I here?" which is the correct attitude. Answers to the word "why" will always mislead and misguide you causing you to go around in circles with no convincing answer anywhere in sight. Your question of "why should energy be destructive?" is not important. Your question of "why did a Hitler exist?" is totally irrelevant.

However, awareness of destructive elements and the "what can be done about it" is relevant. In so recognizing, your first hurdle has been crossed. Your next step would be to send images of light to, yes, even a Hitler. Several such subsidiaries of hate-energy continue to disrupt the work of images of light sent by the mindfully conscious entities on the material and the non-material plane.

It is only with persistence and absolute oneness of mind and attention, which would lead to goal realization. Submit, and you lose faith in the "self," resulting in the subsequent loss of the ideal and victory of the disruptive agencies. Maintain a stance of confidence in the "knowing" and victory is yours. This knowing is faith, the unmistakable stamp of truth, light and knowledge.

The word "why" holds an air of regret in it. The word "what" is positive, with a directness of a fire tipped arrow. The words, "I Am" are more positive than "I will be." Although the "I will" is consciousness itself, here it is used in the context of a postponed action which may or may not take place. The "I Am" on the other hand, causes you to take responsibility as of now, and so act. It is with this attitude of confidence, of knowing who you are, that the process of "becoming" begins.

How often have you introduced yourself to another being as, "I Am," with your name attached to it, yet not really thought about its meaning? The next time you use the words, I Am, in any context, think about what and how you are presenting yourself.

What is it you wish to convey with the "I Am?" You give yourself meaning to names selected by you, yet do not realize what it holds. You give yourself a name, yet fail to understand the "what" of a name. Every thought, thought of, every name uttered, every word presented, carries with it a subtle message which finds its way into the minds of another.

Every being primarily is at war fighting the forces inside of it and trying to discern why and what it is which is in contradiction within itself. Why do no two moments hold the same thought, and the same feeling? Why do no two moments have the sameness of intentions? Why one thought, one moment is good, the other moment negating the same?

Every individual fights a lonely battle within himself/herself in total bewilderment at all the tug and pull of different levels of energy, both inside and outside of a body. Every individual, every being, is essentially good. Evil has not taken up permanent residence in any of you. Fear swallows you and directs you into the performance and non-performance of evil acts. Fear of losing a thing or a person, and several other forms of fear that grips you makes you vulnerable to its dictates. Therefore evil persists. An evil act, is a cowardly act.

It is those who are aware of this fear factor who silently, in communication with the conscious force, set about accomplishing their goal. They understand why a certain act, is performed by a certain individual. In such an understanding they understand energy and defeat the intentions of unwanted energy. These are the individuals who contribute to the good energy circulating in the atmosphere. Now is your time to understand such energy and thus understand the reactions of people and thereby convert bad energy to good.

Let me tell you another secret of the dynamics of thought. In so comprehending the power of thought and perfecting oneself in its proper utilization, the dynamics of non-thought evolves. Have you ever heard of that, dear one?

Do you mean that we then become zombies? Or become like those idyllic cherubs with wings, we as painters love to paint?

You are trivializing thought once again. Zombies listen to the dictates of another thought, which means thought is applied in so complying with another person's thought. Non-thought is a condition whereby the mind stops even the positive thought from occurring. Mind and body reach that oneness with the conscious self, that is me, and thus they dwell only on my thought. This is what you call Utopia. But the time is not yet ripe for such a condition. Your energy has to first be converted to positive energy, and then the condition of non-thought will prevail. That is when you become a "being."

If animate and inanimate beings and things possess consciousness, and consciousness is an energy force, then this amethyst stone on my desk, even as I write this, should be possessing consciousness with some intelligence.

Sure it does, do you doubt it?

Not doubt you, but it just seems bizarre that an object should contain the same intelligence or consciousness that I possess. For a moment let me go with the flow and assume this amethyst stone before me is you or rather you are in it too, can I then communicate with it?

Remember I mentioned about perceptive awareness and awareness of consciousness?

Yes I do. Perceptive awareness is that which the senses perceive, and is aware of but not consciously. Whereas, conscious awareness is being aware by utilizing you or the conscious force.

Very good. Bear with me on that same chain of thought and listen to this. Perceptive awareness is awareness where the senses and the mind are applied, unless the concerned being is aware of consciousness too, and applies me along with perceptive awareness. Then I dance on a perceptive level too. Your amethyst stone for example or any inanimate object, although inherent of consciousness, lacks perception and the sensory organs. Therefore it reflects consciousness devoid of perception. A consciousness in all its purity, without any mind and without any preconceived notions. You might wonder why I keep harping on the dangers of predrawn notions. It is because of judgmental tones that such notions carry. Every notion has an underlined, subtle judgement tone about it. If you were to give such a consciousness devoid of perceptions, a label and a name in a physical world, you would call it "reflective awareness."

Although your stone is devoid of senses, it has potential. Again, try to recall what was mentioned earlier about potential consciousness, kinetic and internalized consciousness. Your stone has potential consciousness that can be utilized and converted to a different level of consciousness through proper channels of energy. This is the magical transformation and transmutation capability of energy.

How does one utilize the potential consciousness of an inanimate object, dear big self of mine? And by the way, does not such uses turn to abusing energy for destruction. Look at what has happened with the Atom. The splitting of Atom has resulted in its abuse.

And do you know what this Atom is? It is the same that is in you and the stone and every rubble you find. This Atom is "Soul." You and all your brethren wish to use Soul to destroy Soul force?

That is what I am trying to convey to you, dear Soul. Will such knowledge of the usage of consciousness in bricks and stones lead to the abuse of it and cause some more devastation? Yes it will. Yet you are imparting such knowledge to me!

Precisely! You are to determine and discriminate construction from destruction. If you are to use an object to destroy, destruction of "self" and every other self is imminent. For you too are a representative of the whole Soul.

Coming back to my amethyst stone here in front of me—you had earlier said that every being is consciousness itself and has to evolve to a perfect state. How then can this stone evolve of its own accord, since it too is consciousness?

It does not evolve; it is a means or can be used as a means for your evolvement. Why just this stone, the ring you have on your person, the bracelet, your watch or whatever is dear to you, becomes personalized with your senses and the mind attaching such importance to it. Now here is the key—depending on your present level of evolutionary stage and the process of your thought, if the outside, similar energy wishes to evoke a certain thought in you, for your further advancement, it enters into it. The stone or object charged with the importance you give it, and the already present consciousness in it along with that energy converted into a subtle being, charging it with its presence, becomes a highly charged entity. It acquires powers, which you call "magical." But make sure that your thoughts are positive, for the overall benefit of the work of the Soul.

You then have a three-way connection between you, the potential consciousness of the stone and the psychic energy. Thus you have a three-way conference call that you can contact and connect without actually dialing. You do not have to rub the stone, like Aladdin and his magic lamp. Your mere invocation or thought of it is sufficient for such a contact to be made.

This is not only getting complicated, but also getting to sound more and more like a fairy tale. By the way, I notice you have dropped your usual tirade of words on me. They now seem to fall gently.

Fairy tales, imaginations and every conceivable idea that the mind images or thinks of, is a possible manifestation. As for the tirade of words falling gently now on your ears, I now have your complete attention and concentration. "Achtung." (Attention) Your are "here and now" with me. Here is something more about entities with energy. As you write each word, you are creating an entity. The more intense your concentration on the creation of such words, the more power these entity words accumulate. Not just the words, but the space between each word vibrates with dynamism, charged by the words flanking it. And when the book is closed, or your computer is turned off, these word entities jiggle with energy with the power so given.

Yes, they get together and have a regular meeting. The next time you consult your book or your computer, it feeds you with an-

other new thought. You then assume that this thought is your own creation. Not so! These entities feed you with more thought. That is if you are open to them and if you are "conscious" to their existence. Negative thought feeds on negative energy and supplies with some more conducive, negative agencies. The next time you are fed with some thought or an idea, which has destructive tendencies, take note of it and gently, but firmly put it away.

Else you will be creating a pattern and before you realize, you will have a matrix of negativity surrounding you.

The dynamics of thought is great, and greater still is the dynamics of non-thought. Any image held in the mind's eye, for a certain period of time, results in its physical manifestation, of that you are aware by now. Even more important is the picture clarity of the image so held and the consistency of it. Streamlined images as opposed to hazy, blurred pictures send a definite pattern in the energy waves converting energy to matter. This is your form of communication with energy. Just as you take a picture of yourself with an instrument that you call "camera," bringing life of another you in another form, similarly through the lens of your mind a picture or an image formed, sends forth signals to waves traversing through space resulting in actual, material manifestation. A manifestation of whatever it is you have expended the energy of your thought on.

Did I not tell you the importance of images? The dynamics of non-thought on the other hand does not involve the mind. I as the Soul do all the imagery. For that, your mind's complete and total surrender to me; your Soul is essential. Use the power of your will to overcome the mind and the dictates of the mind.

For centuries man has battled with one question asked in different ways and means. The one elusive question. "Where is god?" God, O dear vain, little one, is yet to become. That state of perfection is yet to be achieved, for conscious force, although knowledgeable, is not perfect. It is through you and all of you that god can be, that you can be—that you can be god, you can become immortal. While so becoming, your material has to become subtle and less dense to be able to float. Your individuality, as you know it to be, will be lost. What you now perceive through your senses will not be perceived as the same then. In short, the world as you see through these eyes now, will be different then. This is the other dimension that you will be entering.

I shall tell you a parting secret. One last secret! Power of the great or great power, whichever way you wish to put it, is in the small. It is in the weak and those who appear to be helpless. Out of such weakness, such helplessness, shall arise a force so tremendous as would overpower that, which appears mighty. The force of the mighty pushing the weak for a breakthrough will re-

sult in the overflowing of power from the weak, surging and propelling energy upward, thus releasing the tension of the good and the bad to a state of being. A state beyond disparities and contradictions, beyond good and evil.

Go my dear reflection. Set out to the task of becoming, for it is high time, and the time is right. Time is always right, and it waits patiently. Waits until you and all of you realize what it is you "will" to realize—"will" to realize physical immortality. Realize your alignment with the one force, the Soul—to realize and realign yourselves with the Self.

Gently does the rain now fall,
The howling wind, a mere sigh;
It is music I hear in the cry of the jackal,
All fading, well into the night.